Does Religious Education Have a Future?

The place of religion in the modern world has changed significantly over the past two decades. This has been partially reflected in the academic study of religion, but little, if at all, in religious education. In addition, the place of RE in schools has been the subject of intense debate due to changes to the curriculum and school structure, as well as being part of wider debates on religion in the public sphere.

Written by two highly experienced leading practitioners of RE, *Does Religious Education Have a Future?* argues for a radical reform of the subject based on principles of pedagogy set free from religious concerns. It challenges teachers, researchers and educators to rethink their approaches to, and assumptions about, religious education, and enables them to see their work in a larger context that includes pedagogical ideas and political forces.

The book offers readers fresh, provocative and expertly informed critical perspectives on:

- the global context of RE, debates about religion in public places, and religion's response to modernity, violent extremism, science and secularism;
- the evolving educational rationale for RE in schools;
- the legal arrangements for RE and their impact on the teaching of the subject;
- the pedagogy of teaching approaches in RE and their effect on standards and perceptions of the subject;
- the educational commitment of faith/belief communities, and how this influences the performance of RE.

Does Religious Education Have a Future? proposes a new attitude to the subject of religious education, and a new configuration of both its role and content. This book is essential reading for academics, advisers and policy makers, as well as teachers of RE at primary and secondary levels and trainee and newly qualified teachers.

Mark Chater is Director of Culham St Gabriel's, a trust supporting research, development and innovation in religious education. He was senior adviser with responsibility for RE at the Qualifications and Curriculum Authority, and before that, a teacher and trainer of RE.

Clive Erricker is a consultant and researcher in the fields of education and religion. Prior to this, he was County Inspector for Religious Education, History and Community Cohesion in Hampshire, and was previously Head of the School of Religion and Theology and Reader in Religion and Education at the University of Chichester, UK.

Does Religious Education Have a Future?

Pedagogical and policy prospects

Mark Chater and Clive Erricker

Routledge
Taylor & Francis Group

LONDON AND NEW YORK

First published 2013
by Routledge
2 Park Square, Milton Park, Abingdon, Oxon OX14 4RN

Simultaneously published in the USA and Canada
by Routledge
711 Third Avenue, New York, NY 10017

*Routledge is an imprint of the Taylor & Francis Group, an informa
business*

British Library Cataloguing in Publication Data
A catalogue record for this book is available from the British
Library

Library of Congress Cataloging in Publication Data
Chater, Mark, 1956- author.
Does religious education have a future? : pedagogical and policy
prospects / Authored by Mark Chater and Clive Erricker.
pages cm
Includes index.
ISBN 978-0-415-68169-8 (hbk) -- ISBN 978-0-415-68170-4 (pbk)
-- ISBN 978-0-203-11769-9 (ebk) (print) 1. Religious education.
2. Religion and state. I. Erricker, Clive, author. II. Title.
BV1471.3.C43 2013
207'.5--dc23
2012012428

ISBN: 978-0-415-68169-8 (hbk)
ISBN: 978-0-415-68170-4 (pbk)
ISBN: 978-0-203-11769-9 (ebk)

Typeset in Garamond
by Saxon Graphics Ltd, Derby

Printed and bound in Great Britain by
TJ International Ltd, Padstow, Cornwall

To Clive's first grandson, Henry,
and Mark's sons, Michael, Guy and Dominic –
learners of the present and the future.

Contents

Introduction

The politics and discourse of RE

Mark Chater and Clive Erricker

Is this a book about religious education, or about politics? It is both: it is about the future of RE, in which the quality and integrity of its pedagogy is intimately bound up with its local and national structures, influenced by social, legal and religious forces. We start with an assumption that everything that happens in religion, in education and therefore in religious education, is saturated with power relations, many of them undeclared and unexamined. We believe it is necessary to write about RE in this way for two reasons: first, that the English model of RE is characterized by a unique set of discourses, political structures and social norms that influence the quality of its pedagogy and that have served to keep English RE in existence over a period of more than 60 years; and second, that these discourses, structures and norms are now being swept away by a reforming government, with severe consequences for the survival of English RE in its present form. To address RE politically, therefore, seems highly appropriate both as a critical examination of its evolution and claims to educational effectiveness, and also as a response to the present crisis of RE's survival.

But politics, for us, means more than the arrangements for local RE and the legislation that surrounds it. Looking more deeply, RE is governed by political, economic and cultural forces that influence it at every level. These forces work their way from the global level, through national policies and movements of thought, down into classrooms, in a chain of consequence, impacting on the minds of teachers and learners – a chain whose links are largely unexamined, and whose consequences are almost wholly undescribed. It should be the purpose of RE in our time to begin a counter-chain upwards, by initiating a critical exploration and questioning of the words, beliefs and methods that furnish and clothe those power relations, from the classroom to the movements of thought and national structures, and up to the global level of cultural, economic and political forces.

The objection may be made that this would make RE a study of politics, or conflate it with another subject, citizenship. We do believe that RE and citizenship have many shared characteristics, not least some common discourses about values in the public sphere and some challenges in finding a defensible pedagogy. For example, every political, theological or philosophical position constructs its own paradigm; asking questions of any paradigm's logic is the beginning of changing the world. The two subjects also face a current threat of marginalization in the curriculum, and we make proposals about a possible structural relationship between the two that would, we believe, strengthen them both. However, this book is not merely an argument about the similarities between two subjects on the school timetable. It is an invitation to consider what happens in RE in terms of transactions of power; to see each RE classroom as a place where globally manufactured values are marketed to young people; to wonder why so few people seem to notice this, and to ask whether it could and should be different.

In the UK, RE has developed in particular ways since the inception of a post-war settlement in 1944. While there are common characteristics, the subject has evolved under the influences of the four increasingly different jurisdictions of England, Wales, Scotland and Northern Ireland, and the longer-term, less visible but very powerful influences of scholarship in religious studies and pedagogy.[1] Over time, this has produced a diversity of settlements for RE, as for other aspects of school policy. It has long been a matter of consensus that RE in its British model is unique, in particular that its discourses and structural arrangements historically resolve some of the underlying tensions between the study of religion and the representation and inner life of religious traditions and spiritual experience. For this reason, it is true that British RE – and particularly its largest element, the English model – attracts admiring interest from some other national systems.[2] The assumptions that sit behind this admiring interest are worthy of critical examination: for example, that offering young people information about diversity serves to promote harmony and cohesion; that agreed syllabuses and teaching approaches give young people free rein to ask questions and express views; that the localized model of RE protects the subject from undue influence by religious communities or political, economic or cultural forces; that the quality of RE, the rigour of its demand and the relevance of its content, has been successful; that the distinctive construction of RE as 'learning about religion' and 'learning from religion' has helped teachers to plan with educational integrity and coherence. All these assumptions were, we believe, questionable even before the May 2010 election which brought in a coalition government and changed the direction of English RE, and the wider curriculum, irrevocably.

There are factors that make it easier to migrate the English model of RE to other parts of the world: they include information technology, global insights on the impact of religion and belief, and the emerging recognition of fundamentalism in all religions as a generic problem in conflict with modernity, democracy and human rights. However, the success of the English model is itself in contention[3] and the elements of its international success may also disguise the ways in which the model has been failing to fulfil its potential in England, and could continue to fail if planted elsewhere. This book, therefore, could serve as a warning to national jurisdictions of education as to where their interest in English RE might lead them. Some of the most characteristic features of English RE up to this moment, for example its compromises between the interests of religious communities and those of educators, or its balancing act between 'learning about' and 'learning from' religion, should come with a health warning for other national systems. The fact that these features are easily transferred at the press of a button, or appear to be a convenient solution to competing interests in RE, or seem to offer a defence against pressing problems of fundamentalist resurgence, should not blind global educators to the weaknesses. Likewise, some of the dominant discourses of English RE – its approval of tolerance, its treatment of localism as a hoorah-word, its claims of rigour and relevance – deserve a careful search before being imported to other national systems. *Caveat emptor*: the English system and discourses of RE have not worked for us as well as we have sometimes claimed, and they might not withstand the impact of global forces as well as we have sometimes wished.

Religious education has enormous untapped potential. Perhaps its distinguishing feature, its unique selling point, is the critical examination of our inner and outer worlds – of the relations of power that exist in religious and secular movements of thought and in the way our lives and allegiances are organized. Asking questions about the power of ideas and forces is the characteristic which, when present, makes RE vital among curriculum subjects, and when absent, reduces it to convenience and mediocrity.

In writing this book, we draw on our knowledge of international research on RE, spirituality in children and young people, school ethos and leadership. We also use our experience as advisers and policy makers for RE in the English system. Work in the academic, advisory and policy fields has given us experiences that often cannot be documented and published, but which count as source material, being evidence of how a system works or appears to work. What we have seen and learnt in our encounters with children, young people, teachers, academics and other policy colleagues must, we feel, be weighed in argument together with other, published research. But this must be done in a way that is balanced and prevents unfair exposure of individuals or institutions. For the appropriate expression of these insights we have evolved a collection of stories, which appear at the start of most chapters. These stories are not of any one time or place; they are composites, accurately reflecting the patterns we have seen and encapsulating them more neatly than the particulars of reality could. We make no apology for these acts of fiction: we consider them important evidence of a narrative kind, and conveyors of truth. Fictional approaches can make available a range of insights and interpretations that more conventional qualitative and quantitative research approaches might miss. Such a methodology, which is not unknown amongst social scientists and educational theorists,[4] is justifiable in our context because of an ethical need to protect individuals and communities, and also because the task of conveying the multiple complexities of RE's position in the educational world requires an approach that is at once concretely situated and analytically verifiable. We invite readers to use the stories, alongside the other evidence, to interrogate their own experience of RE.

Hazel, a newly promoted teacher of RE, was having a day of contradictions. In the morning, her class of Year 10s (14 and 15-year-olds) stimulated her just as they usually did. In the afternoon, attending a meeting of her local Standing Advisory Council on RE (SACRE) forced her to ask some hard questions.

Her Year 10s – whom she often described as 'brilliant' – had been grappling with the key concept of truth. Hazel let them loose on a collection of statements from the New Testament, the Qur'an, the Adi Granth and Bertrand Russell. After a brief input on the four sources, she set them the challenge of identifying which source they came from, with reasons, and in what ways they were incompatible with each other. Students had to move the statements around on a whiteboard, discussing their reasons with each other and finally presenting their findings to the class. Things were going very well when one group's presentation was interrupted by a single student's question: 'But which one's true?' This provoked heated debate which lasted for the rest of the lesson. 'What do you believe, Miss?' they asked several times. Hazel told them it wouldn't be right for her to influence them by telling of her own beliefs. As they were leaving, Hazel heard one student saying quietly to her friend: 'Well, that was a failure. We didn't find out the true answer.'

That afternoon, as the SACRE was gathering and getting ready to start its meeting, Hazel thought about her students' questions – 'Which one's true?' ... 'What do you believe, Miss?' and blamed herself for failing to engage with them more deeply.

Her thoughts were interrupted by the SACRE Chair, a County Councillor, who wished to make an announcement:

> As you know, ladies and gentlemen, it has been our custom to open these SACRE meetings with a prayer. As today is the turn of our Muslim friend to lead with his prayer, I shall be handing over to the vice-Chair for this part, and I shall wait outside the chamber saying my own prayer to the one I believe to be the true God.

There was a stunned silence as he walked out.

During the two-hour meeting, no one commented on the Councillor's statement. Hazel thought: 'Which one's true? Will my students behave like that in 30 years' time?'

Hazel's story confronts us with a number of challenges. Why did the students think that the purpose of the exercise was to arrive at an agreed notion of truth? Why did they think their teacher's view to be important at the outset? What had they assumed about the subject that made them expect to arrive at what was true, despite disputes over this in the material they read? What does this suggest about what they view as the purpose of education: to provide them with certainties? Would they have asked such a question in other subjects? For example, are they expecting, as they might in mathematics, for there to be one correct answer? Or, if this were a history lesson, would they not expect that the reliability of the answer would depend on argument, interpretation, evidence and the provenance of sources? In these respects should students' expectations in RE differ from those in other subjects? It may be that RE, as Hazel is attempting to teach it, is requiring different skills and perspectives than those they normally encounter in other subjects and that, therefore, they are failing to recognize this. If so, is this because the students haven't been appropriately introduced to the subjects' expectations and purposes? If this is correct, then what are the subject's expectations that should be the basis of its contribution to the curriculum?

The SACRE incident is a ground-level example of the issues and the politics that are present within the subject. Religious belief invades the public space. It could be argued that the SACRE member is acting with integrity or hypocritically (after all SACREs have a duty to promote community cohesion). But, above all, this story illustrates how politics, policy and pedagogy are deeply entwined, as this book will seek to show. Also, in the context and role in which this SACRE member was operating, his actions evidence a clear example of disfunctionality.

The construction of this book

The authors have approached the task of developing the book's argument from their different and overlapping perspectives.

Clive's perspective is that of a teacher who has gained experience in the academic, teacher training and advisory and inspectorate fields. He is particularly concerned with the lack of pedagogical sufficiency in RE, the lack of attention to teacher development and the muddled and often insular thinking that takes place in the RE world. His writings have focused on pedagogy in religious education, children's spirituality in relation to learning, and questioning the overall policy for education in relation to capitalist economics.

Mark's perspective is that of a teacher who has evolved pedagogically, and now understands pedagogy in RE to be a problem of pluralism. There may be limitless pedagogies in RE, but each individual teacher is faced with the challenge of working out his or her pedagogical position with consistency and integrity. The further challenge is to develop a repertoire of pedagogies, to be constructed from an understanding of the subject's claims and its rules of engagement, together with a response to the learners' interests and needs in their local and global context. To this starting-point, Mark adds his interest and occasional writing on spirituality, school ethos and school leadership, and his observation of the national and international developments in RE as a national adviser and policy maker.

The book is organized to give Clive's and Mark's perspectives distinctively, while aiming for a clear line of argument on the ways in which RE needs to change in order to survive. Chapters are written either individually, with a brief response from the other author, or jointly. Thus, we hope, a common sense of purpose is evident.

This book is structured in three parts.

Part I. Representations of religion and education: critical enquiries (Chapters I and 2)

The first two chapters set out our understanding of the context. Clive argues that religious superstructures have an ambivalent attitude to democracy and modernity, and are unaccountable. Mark problematizes educational entitlement as obligation, resulting in mixed messages from governments. These two contextual chapters offer the foundation for our analysis of RE's current position and prospects.

Part 2. Diagnosing RE's pedagogy, provenance and politics (Chapters 3, 4, 5 and 6)

In Chapter 3, Mark charts RE's pedagogical problem from classroom to official documents, proposing that RE's founding principles are weakened by confusion and need to be re-evaluated. This is followed in Chapters 4 and 5 by Clive's critical analysis of the theory of RE, first in phenomenology and new ethnographic approaches, and next in contemporary models, arguing that all these theoretical constructions have made unsatisfactory compromises with the restrictions of Western liberalism. Chapter 6 is Mark's critical view of the political structures and mechanisms of English RE, which have failed to serve RE's educational purposes adequately.

Part 3. The case for a radical transformation of RE (Chapters 7, 8 and 9)

The next three chapters are our joint view of RE's possible future development. Chapter 7 offers a new understanding of pedagogy in RE as a teacher's personal and existential stance, taking into account a wide and complex set of forces. Chapter 8 applies this pedagogical insight to faith communities, challenging them to transform their structures and theologies through education. The final chapter applies the pedagogical challenge to processes of teaching and learning, and to the political task of framing a properly educational rationale for the future of the subject.

The question in the title is capable of many answers, dependent on events and attitudes. As two authors, we do not agree on every detail, but we share a conviction that the RE community – scholarly, professional, confessional, communal; local, national and global – has an urgent duty to address the question and embrace change.

Part I

Representations of religion and education: critical enquiries

Chapter 1

The global context of religion and belief

Clive Erricker

Opening story

In order for Hari to get through this week without being in trouble with teachers, it would be necessary for him to be hypocritical. He had recently started using this word 'hypocritical' a lot: partly because, aged 15, he liked ironically impressing his mates with the word; partly because, being naturally cocky, he could twist his teachers' tails with the concept of hypocrisy; and partly because a more thoughtful and observant side of him had suddenly started noticing hypocrisy all around.

This week, Hari's year group had assembly in the hall every day. They were expected to say 'sorry' for bad things they had done. 'Like what?' he wanted to ask. Teachers led daily 'meditations' saying sorry for world poverty, global warming, malaria and other issues. All the students were expected to say 'Amen'. As they were filing out, Hari was overheard saying, in a loud voice, 'Why should I be sorry for all that stuff? It's not my fault. It sucks, man. Hypocritical.' One teacher took him aside and blamed him for spoiling the atmosphere of the assembly and not taking the issues seriously. Hari was warned to stay silent and behave appropriately in assemblies for the rest of the week, or face an interview with his head of year.

The following day, in media studies, another teacher taught Hari's class about the media coverage of the G8 summit. 'Are they the ones who should be sorry?' he asked, out loud. This was followed by RE, where the teacher explained to them that Jews considered illness and poverty to be God's punishment for sins, and that we should respect this belief even if we disagreed with it. Hari was boiling with questions and objections.

For the rest of the week, Hari tried hard to avoid further outbursts. He was learning to keep quiet when he saw inconsistency and hypocrisy.

What is the problem with hypocrisy and why is it so difficult to avoid when we recognize it so readily? Hari's problem is our problem but it does not exist on just a personal level but a global level. When we seek to avoid contradictions, controversy and complexity in the way we organize education we invite criticisms of hypocrisy from our pupils. This chapter deals with the contradictions that exist between religions, ideologies and democracies that then permeate into our curriculum and affect the attitudes of our pupils. In other words we need to seek to challenge the hypocrisies inherent and implicit in the way we teach our pupils. In the teaching of religion this relates to the way in which we represent it and defend that representation.

Introduction

This chapter considers effects of globalization on religion and belief and examines the extent to which religion as ideology has increasingly played its part in shaping affairs in the modern world. The chapter also considers how religions can seek to evade regulation in order to undermine the jurisdiction of nation states in relation to the former's aims and practices. I refer to this below by showing how religions can be understood as acting analogously to the way in which the financial sector escapes regulation by claiming 'offshore' status or challenging the jurisdiction of nation states and international rights legislation, which itself is not free of problems. This is related to the idea of capital, and different forms of capital which, it is argued, concerns the way in which religions and other ideologies do or do not contribute to the overall social fabric and democratic goals as opposed to seeking their own specific and exclusive aims.[1]

Religious resurgence: religious ideology and religion as a reactionary force

The resurgence of religion has reaffirmed its significance in the affairs of the modern world. In particular this phenomenon is bound up with questions concerning legitimacy, power and influence, jurisdiction, conflicts in values and worldviews, and religions as political agents.

This resurgence is attested to in the sociology of religion, where the long affirmed thesis of secularization is now contested, thus influencing the trajectory of the discipline.[2] In the nineteenth century religion declined in influence largely because its influence waned as a form of social utility within Europe and the UK. The Methodist dissenters used literacy as a means to their cause; the Salvation Army used the practice of addressing dissolute behaviour as a means to theirs. Today these issues are addressed by other means. However, the repair of the social fabric by religious means is alive and well in other areas of the world. In Iran it brought about the revolution in 1979. In parts of Africa it is entwined with post-colonial renewal. Meanwhile, suspicion of imperialist intentions by the democratic West is also resurgent because of its alignment with capitalism creating a narrative of continuing post-colonial exploitation. This has to be taken seriously since, for example, the evidence reveals that 'offshore' and deregulated financial activity exceeds by tenfold the amount in aid that is given to Africa.[3] It is in this context that a resurgence of militant religious movements across the world needs to be understood partly as a response to the rapacious activity of some Western interests. It is also in this respect that the policy of Western states with regard to the Middle East, the criticism of terrorist activity, the actions of al-Qaida, the war on Iraq and military activity against the Taliban in Afghanistan and the attempt to democratize the country need to be understood in relation to a contra-narrative that benefits violent or threatening movements that oppose the Western interests. Just as, in the twentieth century, fascism's and communism's political prominence and subsequent demise were central to the script of that century, so will religious resurgence and militancy be in that of the twenty-first. The tensions reside not just in the material issues of democratic rights, human rights, women's rights, homophobia and other often reported incidents but in what gives rise to the possibility of and justification for the contra-narrative. There is an antagonism toward the hegemony of Western capitalist hubris and exploitation and scepticism toward the democratic narrative. Anti-democratic nation states and religious systems wish to prevent themselves being subjected to Western democratic-capitalist regulation that is likely to interfere with their own authority, interests and practices.

As examples of these, if we examine Vatican Roman Catholicism and Iranian Shia Islam, we can recognize that they are both genuinely hierarchical and autocratic in that the truth (knowledge) can only be discerned by those trained to do so: the Congregation for the Doctrine of the Faith, the Holy See, and pontifical authority, on the one hand, and the Ulema and Ayatollahs (jurists) on the other. This is reflected in the fact that their theologies are the basis of legal systems. As a result, both are also genuinely anti-democratic. Such systems, by virtue of their truth being universally valid, are also, necessarily, imperialist. There was disappointment in Iran that the Shia revolution failed to export (it was, of course, opposed by the Saudis who feared a loss of their power). The Vatican still sees the enemy to its power and influence as secularism. In Russia the Orthodox Church is a national church; in particular it flourished under Tsar Peter the Great in the eighteenth century when it, in effect, became a state department dealing with education and social welfare. Under the Soviet system it was repressed in its influence but was still used as a state representative with a national and international agenda at international peace conferences. In the post-soviet world it is resurgent. As Irena Mayniak observes, 'The Russian Church falls more naturally into an autocratic order than a democratic one. Pluralism, tolerance, diversity and a global perspective do not form part of its frame of reference.'[4]

Whilst in Europe the model of state–church partnership was the established historical example, in the United States distance was created between state and church; numerous protestant movements flourished, but these were often of a literalist and fundamentalist kind. You could say that this has been an interesting effect of deregulation within a democracy and that it provides a certain parallel with the deregulation afforded to business and finance in the United States. One result of this, however, has been the reactionary views expressed by many of these groups over numerous human rights issues. Two of the most prominent of these have concerned homosexuality and the role and rights of women. These have even affected the Episcopalian Church, with the appointment of a homosexual bishop in liberal New Hampshire and a woman as Presiding Bishop-elect of the Episcopal Church in 2006. These incidents have even provoked congregations to seek new leadership from bishops in Africa who are better disposed to their non-liberal views. The dilemma of democratic rights and religious freedom is a vexed one for liberals, with increasing examples either putting the law to the test or resulting in a determination by secular states to change the law.[5]

Perhaps the most severe test to date of liberal democracy was Khomeini's *fatwa* against Salman Rushdie. This set a precedent. It was the first to be delivered whose jurisdiction extended beyond Muslim countries.[6] In effect it was a reverse strategy in the offshore game: extend your jurisdiction into foreign territory. Iran's Islamic revolution in 1979 also introduced a new and contested interpretation of the concept of *velayat-e faqih* whereby Khomeini himself became the supreme jurist and obedience to his rulings was tantamount to obedience to government, a religious obligation on the population.[7] This is, of course, incompatible with democracy. It also provides something of a parallel to the Vatican claiming its suspected paedophile priests should not be subjected to the laws of nation states. These events are not just about refusing to acknowledge a need to collaborate with democratic nation states and their legislation, but about being opposed to the imposition of law devised by democratic nation states or the international community.

Sarah Maitland provides an interesting commentary on the contradictions inherent within the European enlightenment and democracy that is pertinent to our discussion. 'What I see ... is a faltering, a loss of faith, in the whole Enlightenment project.'[8] Due to the Enlightenment, 'At the political level, [religious sentiment] was replaced by nationalism.'[9] 'Part of the underlying importance of The Satanic Verses episode was the way it exposed the fact that Articles 18 and 19 in the UN Charter of Human Rights were incompatible: it proved impossible to defend both freedom of speech and the right to have one's religious belief and practice respected.'[10] The same is also true of Article 26, which states both that 'Education shall be directed ... to the strengthening of respect for human rights and fundamental freedoms ... shall promote understanding, tolerance and friendship among all nations, racial and religious groups' and 'the maintenance of peace.' But 'Parents have a prior right to choose the kind of education that shall be given to their children.'[11]

What this also teaches us is that the international context is paramount. What happens in any specific national environment is necessarily influenced by the global one and vice versa. While specific nations clamp down on movement into their borders, they are not in control of the influence of religion globally and the type of religion entailed. It is very complex. This is why suicide bombers can be recruited from European countries and why such events as 9/11 can occur in New York and the July 2005 bombings can occur in London. National and religious allegiances do not conform to the same pattern and types. Religious allegiances vary according to international influences and these influences involve different juridical policies and practices.

For example, the Vatican, by virtue of its 'offshore' religious and legal status, rivals the City of London in its 'offshore' financial status as the most deregulated 'state' in the world. Geoffrey Robertson's book *The Case of the Pope: Vatican accountability for human rights abuse* documents the basis on which the Vatican can ignore statutory legal demands by virtue of its unique status as a state and the juridical rights that entails. There are two means by which the Vatican ensures its privileged authority: canon law and its statehood. With regard to canon law it sought to oppose the jurisdiction of the laws of nation states in relation to suspected paedophile priests. Robertson records:

> In 2001, the Vatican actually congratulated Bishop Pierre Pican of Bayeux for refusing to inform police about a paedophile priest and for giving him parish work despite his confession of guilt. ... This came to light after the priest had been sentenced to 18 years for repeated rapes ... and the bishop received a three month suspended sentence for not reporting the abuse, contrary to French law.[12]

Canon Law operates differently from normal law enforcement. It is, in Robertson's words, 'not "law" in any real sense ... but rather a process relating to sins for which the only punishment is spiritual'.[13] This provided the justification behind the scandal within which paedophile priests were protected from legal action as long as the Vatican refused to identify them and submit them to secular legal procedures within the countries in which they committed their offences. This enraged populations of Western nation states because the Church was so reluctant to allow the imposition of secular law in relation to its priests and so reluctant to apologize. The refusal to apologize or take responsibility is a characteristic trait of 'offshore' organizations. A similar tactic has been used by banks following the 2008 financial collapse. They always claim they are a special case and that the normal rules and moral codes do not apply.

The Vatican was granted statehood through the Lateran Treaty in 1929 by Mussolini. The qualifications for statehood of the Montevideo Convention on Rights and Duties of States in 1933 effectively ruled out the statehood of the Vatican[14] but it is still recognized as a state by the United Nations in so far as it retains privileges that other religious bodies and NGOs do not have, specifically in relation to lobbying UN members, and especially through consular relations. These privileges ensure that it is the only 'non-member state' at the UN 'with every entitlement of a member except the right to vote at the General Assembly and to be elected to the Security Council'.[15] Such is its comparative influence and its protection.

There are significant controversies over a number of other issues concerning how religions often act as reactionary forces in the modern world. Those concerning women priests, homosexuality, human and women's rights and contraception in relation to Aids in Africa are pertinent examples. These are not just about the influence of Roman Catholicism but also the influence of specific other Christian churches and forms of Islam, in particular. In some cases, such as female circumcision, we are faced with the conundrum of religion versus 'tribal culture'. It is not just a matter of condemning religious views when they are opposed to progressive liberal opinion but of weighing the doctrines, justifications, causes and consequences of difference and the moral implications involved, and recognizing the socio-political contexts within which these issues exist.

To claim religion is a reactionary force is not to suggest that all forms of religious expression are so, or that all are the same in this respect. For example the Society of Friends (Quakers) and Unitarians could be presented as obvious exceptions. Also, Bahias operate as an inclusive organization, though they certainly have a mission for conversion. Guru Nanak is an earlier example of someone who started a movement that opposed the doctrinalization of religion. All of these movements have suffered persecution at the hands of other religious ideologies but all three have institutionalized into movements with exclusive identities. It is also the case that religions have charitable arms that operate to alleviate suffering and poverty. Nevertheless, these are often subsidiary organizations in tension with the doctrinal and ideological purposes of those branches of religion of which they are a part. CAFOD and Christian Aid serve as particular examples. What is clear is that religion has both ideological and reactionary forms of expression and can sometimes have more liberal ones. We are dealing with a spectrum of characteristics. When these characteristics collide in one religion it is salutary to see what happens, as the liberation theologian Leonardo Boff reports:

> Twenty years ago, on 7 September 1984, I sat on the very same seat as Galileo Galilei [condemned to imprisonment for heresy in 1633] and Giordano Bruno [burned at the stake for heresy in 1600] in the Palace of the Holy Office in Rome – formerly the Inquisition – to defend the opinions expressed in my book *Church, Charism and Power*. ... Twenty years on, I see that there was something providential in what happened to me. ... People discovered another type of Church, denuded of power, simple and prophetic; one that identifies with the poor and shares the denigration and persecution of which they are victims.[16]

However, the church that Boff opposed has continued to retain its power and has limited the impact of liberation theology as a result of its opposition to it.

The above example leads us to a deeper question: what distinguishes different types of religious movements? If we understand democracy to be built on the principles of reason, equality, human rights, toleration and free speech, then any movement that is in tension with such principles is potentially anti-democratic in its ideology. It makes sense, therefore, that such movements should not be given positions of power and influence within democratic states. A democratic state, by definition, has a duty of care to its citizens based on the above principles. Thus, one has to identify those movements that would disrupt the implementation of these principles within a nation state or internationally. It is clear that some religions and varieties of specific religions fall into this category and others do not; thus there are different religious responses to a new law on civil partnerships being conducted within places of worship (including same sex partnerships), for example.[17] Clearly, Vatican Roman Catholicism, some influential varieties of Islam and Fundamentalist and Literalist Christian movements are likely to be the controversial ones (though they are not alone). This is because their epistemologies are at odds with democratic principles. They affirm revelation over reason and their idea of truth is absolutist and unquestionable. Their polity is also anti-democratic; being consistent with their epistemology, they are autocratic, hierarchical and opposed to change. Furthermore, they view the world around them as a threat to them and are unceasingly dogmatic and antagonistic to its culture of secularism and rights, viewing themselves as the victims. Interestingly, there is a similarity between these religious anti-democratic ideologies and others that democratic states have spawned themselves as controversial offspring. Thus, we have the rampant free-market ideology which also resents and rejects any need to operate according to the democratic principles cited above and believes it has no duty of care to the residents of democratic nation states, or to those of other nation states either. It is the mentality of these ideological movements that we should fear, and certainly we should not give them a foothold in our institutional life. And yet we have invited them into our education system such that we are now tendering out schooling to these bodies as part of the deregulation of education (now on the basis of competitive tender). Of course, Roman Catholicism along with the Church of England and some Jewish schools had, historically, gained this foothold previously.

I can recount a small story of my own, relating to a Church of England rural primary school in Hampshire, that illustrates the sort of distortion to democratic enquiry in schools that ideological tensions can cause. I had helped the teacher coordinating religious education redesign the curriculum around conceptual enquiry. She then briefly explained this to the Chair of the Governors, who was also the parish priest, who was present at the end of the day before I left. Near the end of her exposition, with regard to a Year 6 unit of work, he questioned the concept of myth being used in relation to Christian material. In a high-handed way he requested a dictionary, looked up 'myth' and pronounced that a myth was something that was untrue. Therefore, he argued, this particular unit of work should use material from another religion (any one would do) rather than Christianity. What was so distressing was that he didn't even understand the educational principle underpinning an open enquiry (as to what constituted a 'myth', whether the material was 'mythical' and whether and in what sense myths could be said to be 'true'). This is a small example of ideological distortion interfering with an open educational process. For a more detailed and larger argument on this issue see Philip Pullman's essay on theocracies and democracy.[18]

You might well say that this priest/chair of governors was justified, given that the beliefs of the church should be upheld in a church school. But this presents us with a contradiction between the interests of the religious authorities, as articulated by one individual in a position of power, and the educational processes paid for by a democratic state. If you want a free-market version of education in which we can have religious competition for running schools, that sounds like a very different sort of democracy to me: one in which religions have their own 'offshore' status in relation to the way in which democratic principles apply.

Religious migration: militancy, integration and globalization

When religiously infused cultures migrate to the West they seek to bring with them, or attempt to recreate, specific forms of social capital[19] that underpin their identity. These can often be in tension with Western customs and values. The great fear is often that of assimilation; this fear can lead to ghettoization – separate but parallel lives and a lack of economic prosperity, as has been recorded by Sanjay Suri, amongst other studies.[20] The way in which these tensions are addressed will depend on government policy; hence, for example, the multiculturalist policies that Holland and the UK have pursued and contrasting ones in France and Germany. The change in socio-political climate brought about by the events of 9/11 in the United States, the London bombings in 2005, the Madrid bombings, the demonstrations against cartoons of Mohammed in Denmark, other demonstrations elsewhere and the killing of Theo Van Gogh suggest that multiculturalist policies have not been entirely successful.[21] The shift in political climate in Holland has been the most significant evidence of this as the political landscape in Holland moves to the right. The previous attempts by Tony Blair's government in the UK to insist religions modernize does not seem to have brought the outcome desired, as the realization that Britain has produced its own 'home-grown' suicide bombers attests. David Cameron's speech in Munich, Germany, in February 2011, suggests a change in direction in this respect.[22] A tendency to disaffection amongst some young Muslims in Britain also suggests that they are finding their sense of Muslim identity elsewhere than within the communities in which they have grown up. Ed Husain's *The Islamist*[23] sheds some light on that. He states:

In the multicultural Britain of the 1980s and 1990s we were free to practise our religion and develop our culture as we wanted. Our teachers left us alone, so long as we didn't engage in public expressions of homophobia or intimidation of non-Muslims.[24]

As a result, he records the infiltration of the Wahabis (financed by the House of Saud, in a relationship extending back to the eighteenth century) through Jamat-e-Islami into the East London Mosque, which he attended, and the recruitment of the youth to a militant form of Islam.[25] This infiltration extended further. Dr Abdul Bari, one of those who led the mosque committee with allegiance to Jamat-e-Islami, 'later became a leader of the Muslim Council of Britain, while chair of the East London Mosque and Islamic Forum of Europe' whilst a fellow leader of the East London Mosque, Chowdhury Mueen Uddin, 'chaired Muslim Aid'.[26]

Husain further recounts that: 'Cut off from Britain, isolated from the Eastern culture of our parents, Islamism provided us with a purpose and place in life. More importantly, we felt as though we were pioneers, at the cutting edge of this new global development of confronting the West in its own backyard.'[27] The rationale behind the activity of the activists of Jamat-e-Islami and, more radically, Hizb ut-Tahir was to establish a Muslim state to replace democracy and corrupt Muslim governments; it would be a new caliphate based on Islamic law (sharia) with global effect.[28]

By way of contrast, it is worth considering the example of one moderate Muslim group, the Khoja Shia Ithna-sheeris. I have worked with and researched this group over the last 20 years. The aim of the leadership of their worldwide federation is expressed as follows in excerpts from the rationale of its validation document to train new religious leaders on an MA programme validated by an English university:

> The Community vision is to develop as a justly balanced practising Muslim community in keeping with the teachings of the faith and to become useful members of the wider society and engender a sense of belonging and a desire to socially integrate with the society.[29]
>
> However, with globalization and a fluid social structure, together with the dispersal of community members to various parts of the world, there is a growing realization that the cohesive societies that functioned so effectively as close knit communities in India and in Africa, from where they originated, have since lost their impact. This is particularly noted in the West and among community members settled in Australasia. There is growing concern that in this post-modern age, prospects for the continuation of tightly knit traditional communities are quickly waning.
>
> Furthermore, attempts by the older generations at re-living their past and in applying traditional practices to address current challenges faced by a younger generation brought up in the new environments have proved

largely ineffective. Among the younger generation, particularly those born and bred in the West, there is growing disenchantment towards such traditional practices. As a result, they find it increasingly difficult to adhere to such a traditional outlook and to understand practices that they find difficult to relate to within the wider societies in which they live.[30]

The challenge facing the Community is to ensure that their progeny, while acquiring higher education and living away from the traditional Islamic environments, are able to engage with a wider multi-religious and multicultural society whilst successfully maintaining their Islamic values as practising Muslims.[31]

The demands of the post-modern era require generic *Muballigheen* [religious leaders] who can effectively communicate both linguistically as well as contextually to address contemporary dynamics and needs.

This realization has resulted in prompting a number of students from the Khoja Shia Ithna-Asheri community to enroll in various Islamic seminaries in England, Pakistan, India, Iran and Syria. However these seminaries of Islamic learning tend to have little understanding of the particular needs of the Khoja Shia Ithna-Asheri Community.[32]

In the MA programme for training religious leaders mentioned above, four modules were included on relevant Islamic perspectives and two 'Western' modules, on religious teaching and ethics. The inclusion of the latter two modules has been questioned by significant figures within the World Federation on the basis that they are not relevant to the needs of religious leaders. Also, the more traditional programmes for religious training have recruited healthily whilst this programme has struggled to recruit. One of its other progressive but controversial features is that it seeks to recruit married couples, men and women, who can both operate as religious leaders within a community and are taught side by side. Should the Western modules be dropped this rationale would be invalidated and the university validation of it would cease.

In teaching one of the 'Western' modules on this programme, in one session I asked the students to consider who were their role models. All named their parents but one also named Ayatollah Khomeini, the instigator of the Iranian revolution who pronounced a *fatwa* [ruling] against Salman Rushdie, after which Rushdie was a target of death threats. The reason he named Khomeini, he said, was that the Ayatollah stood up for the need for Islam to oppose Western interests, which made him an iconic figure in the resurgence of Islam. This particular student went to school with Mohammad Sidique Khan, one of the four 2005 London suicide bombers, who was brought up in Beeston, Yorkshire. However, the student was genuinely perplexed as to why Khan became an Islamic militant. The point is that the student was not enamoured of militant Islam but he still admired Khomeini. He was not alone in this sentiment, as Malik records in quoting Inayat Bunglawana, now a leading figure in the Muslim Council of Britain; when Ayatollah Khomeini issued the *fatwa*, Bunglawana states, 'I felt a thrill. It was incredibly uplifting. The imam addressed "Proud Muslims" and I felt proud myself. It transformed the power equation. I no longer felt isolated. Muslims were standing up for themselves.'[33] Malik notes that this reaction, born of the frustration of disempowerment, was paralleled in white working-class labour voters and activists who had turned to the BNP, 'They listen to us. ... No one else does. And they stand up for the white man. ... What's racist about standing up for yourself.[34]

The KSI has approximately 100,000 adherents worldwide. It is committed, amongst its leadership, 'to a wider multi-religious and multicultural society'. It has aspiring leaders from, for example, Leeds and Los Angeles, who are also firmly committed to their Muslim identity and that of their respective local communities. It is as good as it gets for the project of community cohesion. But, compare the KSI's adherents with the number of Muslims worldwide and those in the West and you start to see the scale of the political problem when such an initiative as this is not in place for other Muslim communities and is even contested within its own.[35] The perceived lack of need by Muslim organizations in the West to have religious leaders who can communicate effectively with those outside their communities and contribute to mutual understanding and cohesion is a worrying feature. It suggests that the idea of standing up for yourself, whilst maintaining a separate identity, may persist rather than being replaced with a greater sense of inclusive belonging.

This does not have to be the case. Grand Ayatollah Ali-Al-Sistani, Iraq's leading Shia cleric, and the one that the KSI go to for *taqleed* (juridical advice or *fatwas*), recognizes the UN as the 'embodiment of international legality'.[36] He regards Shia Islam as 'in essence a democratic ideal, especially as laid out in the charter crafted by the fourth caliph Imam Ali in the seventh century'.[37] He has opposed the *velayat-e faqih* doctrine (the guardianship or vice-regency of an Islamic jurist within Shia Islam) as interpreted by Khomeini and has given his consent to interfaith marriage. In Iraq it has been said by Iraq's president, Ghazi Alyawer, that 'Al-Sistani is our guarantee of democracy.'[38] He is the leader of Iraq's 12 million Shias and of many more worldwide, sometimes in migrant situations.

When we consider change occurring within migrant religious communities, forms of capital are the catalyst. Taking the KSI as an example we can note that religious capital, maintaining their own Shia identity, has always been a priority. They are a comparatively affluent group, valuing educational success and identifying professional status as important. Typically they have entered accountancy and pharmacy as the most chosen professions. However, with generational change, the maintenance of religious identity as a priority has weakened. At the same time economic capital has become more important for the youth. Having been brought up in comfortable middle-class homes they seek to improve their lives through lucrative employment. At the same time their ties to religious identity diminish. This is the first or second generation born in the West and they lack the same cultural connections outside that culture that their parents or grandparents previously had.

By contrast, a study of Pure Land Japanese Buddhists who migrated to California showed no doctrinal allegiance in the second generation to Japanese Pure Land Buddhism; it was a cultural form that they showed some allegiance to by attending festivals but it had no religious resonance in relation to their identity. By the third generation, and second US-born, the residue of Buddhist values most often meant they were more concerned with general values issues which bound those of different faiths and none within American society. Any residue of Buddhism was not related to the specific form of Japanese Buddhism of the previous generations but to forms of American Buddhism, more eclectic in kind.[39]

This tells us something quite significant. Whereas the Japanese study showed that cultural and ethnic identity was initially most important and transmitted through the means of a particular form of Buddhist identity, in the Islamic case it was specifically the religious identity that mattered and the cultural and ethnic identity less so. If we can tentatively generalize the point, Buddhists do not usually tend to regard their identity as being focused on religious ideology but Muslims do to a greater extent. For the latter the loss of religious identity is of paramount concern. They are not necessarily averse to capitalism *per se*, but secular capitalism is another matter. I accept that here I am painting with a broad brush and am seeking only to identify a general characteristic.

My own study of a Buddhist primary school in Brighton, Sussex tends to bear out the distinction in my analysis above.[40] Whilst it is wholly committed to Buddhist values it has no concern about children becoming Buddhist in any religious or ideological sense. One of the main messages I am seeking to convey in this chapter is that broad-brush terms such as relations between religion, culture and ethnicity are not precise enough for us to determine how they affect community or global cohesion. What is more important is to recognize the various relationships between religion and ideology and the way these impact on group and individual identity. This has a significant effect on whether religious groups are happy to assimilate or integrate or are determined to remain 'offshore'.

In order to understand the place and role of religion in a globalized world we have to start by realizing that the global world is made up of a number of ideologies in tension with one another; some of these are religious and others not. Therefore, the overarching category within which we have to place religions is ideologies. Some ideologies are more benign, and others are aggressive. Religions fall into both categories, as do differing secular ideologies. We might wish to characterize differing religions and beliefs as belonging in one category or the other: for example, we might wish to say that humanism and Unitarianism are more open to democratic and inclusive principles, while free-market capitalism, neo-liberalism, fundamentalism and several instances of authoritarian propositional monotheism have a profound antipathy to democracy. However, the reality is that most concrete manifestations of religion and belief find themselves in both categories at once, depending on variations of place, denomination and generation. This reality is explored further in Chapter 8, where Mark develops the concept of the educational economy of ideological communities. Another way of understanding this is to think in terms of the traditional Christian theological distinction between apologetics and dogmatics. Apologetics is 'anthropological' in its arguments and seeks to appeal to non-believers; dogmatics rests on the idea of the unique truth of God's revelation, which acts as a fundamental criticism of the mode of society in place and/or a dismissal of the same as irrelevant. As examples we can compare Schleiermacher's *Speeches on Religion to its Cultured Despisers*[41] and Paul Tillich's works[42] with Karl Barth's Commentary on the *Epistle to the Romans*[43] and his *Church Dogmatics*.[44] Another way of making the distinction is by determining which movements are genuinely democratic and which are strictly (sometimes covertly) authoritarian, hierarchical and exclusivist.

Conclusion

This chapter has been concerned with the way in which specific branches or organizations within a religion can be differentiated and classified on the basis of being ideologies that oppose democratic principles and organization. The argument presented is that these represent threats to democracies. At the same time, I have argued that there are specific ideologies that exist within democracies that are threats of a similar kind, such as free-market capitalism. They have in common that they seek 'offshore' status within which they are not subject to democratic regulation. At the same time they can be geographically either onshore or offshore. As a result we start to see the impact of globalization: it is both at home and abroad. Nation states are subject to both international and domestic influences that are interconnected. The major point is that it is not religions per se with which we should be concerned but international global, national and local ideologies, of which certain religious movements form a part and are major players. In turn this influences the way in which forms of capital are accumulated, influential and politically significant in terms of their appropriation within and beyond democratic governance. We shall see, in later chapters, how this influences education and religious education and why our present provision is unable to adequately reflect this state of affairs in its curriculum representation of religion.

We must take account of Hari's point on hypocrisy made at the beginning of this chapter. Our representation of religion, and of values, must be honest, reflect complexity and be open to scrutiny. If a teacher states that religion is a force for good and then selectively provides images of religion that support that view, that would be no more trustworthy than another teacher saying all religion is bad. The point is to engage with the complexity of the phenomenon and not censor out subject matter in order to simplify it, protect it or dismiss it. Additionally, expressions of religion must be studied in relation to their socio-cultural contexts (they have never existed outside such a context), not extrapolated from them as though they are somehow on a higher plane. We might say, using a photographic metaphor, don't trust the teacher who just uses a high-magnification zoom lens to provide information upon which pupils can only arrive at a conclusion that is within that frame of reference. It is also necessary to provide the wide-angle shots that reveal the unedited messy complexity for scrutiny.

In the following chapter we ask questions about education within this conflicted state of affairs in relation to the purposes of schooling and the design of curricula. Education is problematized not in relation to religion or religious education specifically, but in the way we situate ourselves within an educational response to a contemporary dilemma as to how we can best prepare and support young people to be effective agents in the modern world, in which religion still has an influential role.

Response from Mark Chater

Clive's chapter raises vital questions for educators: how much does the misbehaviour of some religious authority structures matter? Is it possible to distinguish the anti-democratic, unaccountable practices of some religious authorities from the more humble, accessible and honestly searching lifestyles adopted by some leaders and many followers worldwide? How would one begin to draw up a balance sheet of the comparative influences of the former and the latter? How can and should religious educators take account of these tensions? How can they be presented in classrooms?

In 2011, people camped outside many financial institutions in major cities, protesting against the unaccountability of global capitalism and the moral failure of the banks. London, home to the great cathedral of St Paul's in the heart of the financial district – 'the City' – has been witness to an encampment outside the cathedral's main doors. Their presence provoked a crisis in the cathedral community itself, leading to the resignation of two senior priests and much internal debate on how the cathedral and the wider church should respond. While some church leaders have welcomed the encampment as a prophetic critique of Western economics and of the church, others have sought to use the law to remove them, arguing from the church's institutional interests and exonerating the church from any direct responsibility for the banking crisis.[45] The debate has asked questions that enable people to reach the heart of Christianity: what would Jesus do, have Christians prioritized their institutions at the expense of their gospel, how can people and communities change? It is fair to say that the provocation of these events has been an occasion of learning for the church, and could be seen as a gift.

In these events, and others similarly affecting many different communities of religion and belief, do we have something applicable to religious education? Can such events be the occasion for reaching to the heart of a religion or belief, understanding it better through the prism of a moral crisis? Or will it transpire that in a time of fear, enquiry into difficult issues is closed down by the forces of private certainty?

Chapter 2

The conflicted context of education

Mark Chater

Opening story

Young people aged 14–25, from several Western countries, were interviewed in 2011 on how they want to improve their school education. Among their responses were:

- Allow us to ask 'why are we learning this?'
- Ask us what our passion is – value what lies deeper.
- Teach and learn with head, heart and hands.
- Offer academic credits for volunteering.
- See the unique potential of each individual: this is the foundation of resilience.
- Develop more inter-disciplinary projects.
- Make things. Make growth, make beauty, make history, make change.
- I feel I don't question things enough. I might challenge some people a bit more at school. Education is about learning, not just about grades.
- All through my education, teachers have just been telling me, drumming it into me, that if I don't get my grades ... We get told every day that if we don't get the grades, we're going down the drain and not worth anything. The message is too loud, too much.
- Grades right now are really important. There isn't any other way of doing it. We are being trained to get this grade, and then when we've finished we are trained to get the next grade.
- The teachers want the grades. They need the results. Stop there being so much fear in the system. All the teachers are scared of students getting bad grades.
- Stop the conveyor belt.

Introduction

Why do we have publicly funded, free universal education in Western societies, and what amount of influence in it do parents and children expect to have? The voices of young people in the story on the previous page show us that, at the very least, all is not well in the power relations between learners, the curriculum and school accountabilities. This chapter examines the assumptions behind our free universal provision in relation to schooling and the curriculum in the context of a global financial crisis. It asks a number of child-like, or learner-like, questions which lead on to a critical consideration of the role played by compulsory education. Arguing that free universal education is a conflicted and self-contradictory business, the chapter concludes with some notes on the implications those contradictions have for RE, which sits outside the national curriculum structure in England but is strongly influenced by it.

Why go to school, and what happens if I don't?

Families prepare their children for going to school in various ways. In countries where the school is a ten-mile walk away or more, preparation concerns the direct physical tasks of reaching the school safely and on time. In some urban landscapes where the journey to school is shorter but more dangerous, there may be a focus on the choices about a route taken and the strategies for a safe journey. Prosperity brings other agendas: preparation for the journey is focused on the right books and equipment, and the right frame of mind. At home, rituals may attend the first day of the child's school career, the first day back each year, the last day; thus going to school acquires a mystique, sometimes of pride, sometimes of terror, that is reinforced both by authority structures in the school and by economic realities in the surrounding community.

Even though global contexts of schooling vary greatly, there pertains a nearly universal belief in the high priority value of going to school. This has come about partly by the moral and political force of milestone international declarations of human rights.[1] Such declarations enumerate the obligations of states not only to enforce the right to education in legal terms but also to take administrative, judicial, economic and social steps to back it up. In these declarations and the legislation that flows from them, education is recognized as both a fundamental human right in itself, and as a means of securing and defending other human rights.[2] Amongst democratically minded educators it has been rarely questioned, although critiques of the state's compelling role do exist.[3]

We inhabit a very wide consensus that a child's right to education should be a priority in all states. Supporting the consensus, there is an implied belief that the right to education is a particular hallmark of democratic states that respect human rights, diversity and the rule of law. The discourses attendant on this priority are many: for example, that education is every child's right; that human rights and dignity are served by education; that parents and states have an obligation to provide free universal education; that a public education service is a good investment for states; and that education must develop a child's personality. These discourses reinforce the point unanimously that universal education is to be valued positively. The unanimity is remarkable, but it masks confusion.

The frequent repetition that education is important drowns out those voices that ask: why go to school, what is the purpose of education, does and can that purpose change as political priorities change? The purpose of going to school, and the measures of success in a national school system, have not been defined with any unanimity, and remain highly conflicted. This weakness was pointed up in Tim Oates' critique of British curriculum policy as too domestic and introverted.[4] His call for British policy on the curriculum and assessment to pay more attention to successful jurisdictions elsewhere in the world, and to prioritize policy coherence, has been influential on current policy in relation to the curriculum and schools in England. Yet Oates' critique does not go far enough: he saw the confusion, but was content to refer to others equally confused.

If the question is why go to school, many of the popular answers employ a form of circular reasoning that fails to convince. To be educated, to acquire knowledge, to gain good grades, to develop skills, to find a job, to earn a living: for many young people, these reasons may seem convincing enough to repeat them frequently to their elders. Ivan Illich, in his critique of universal compulsory education, suggested that societies believe they 'need' education because of an 'assumption of scarcity', e.g. scarcities of jobs, resources, creativity or excellence; and for any of these scarcities the 'cure' is a socially constructed 'good' called education.[5] His belief placed the education system in the wider context of capitalist societies in which scarcity and surplus were, and still are, constantly generated. In times of recession, the economic and instrumentalist reasons for going to school tend to be repeated even more forcefully, with warnings that a less well educated, or perhaps we should say less well qualified, person has fewer life chances. Yet many young people recognize that the promises cannot be true for them all, and speak of a time, place and priority that is not immediate to them. At age 15, what does it matter to me that adults know the benefits of a good education, if I do not believe it works for me, if I am afraid to risk it or fail to make use of it? What does it matter to be told that an educational failure is more likely to become homeless, jobless or pregnant too early, or to die young? These drastic narratives of ultimate scarcity make poor advertisements for an education system if that is its only, or main, selling point.

If the question behind 'Why go to school?' is 'What is the purpose of my education?' – and many young people want to know this, though not all can articulate the question – then the narrative offered by the school and wider society, the story behind the aims and purposes of schooling as expressed to the young, matters enormously. In many developed countries we have become hesitant or negligent about articulating the aims of schooling to our young people. We have lived for a century or more with a system that provides schooling for all, and expects all to make use of it; perhaps we have reached the point of taking it for granted.

Compulsory universal schooling can be understood as a major form of what Pierre Bourdieu terms cultural capital.[6] It is capital because it uses money to purchase something whose value is as powerful and transferable as money; it is cultural because it buys a cultural norm, an ideal – the educated human being, the educated society. This purchased ideal is underpinned by a set of doxa or beliefs: for example that we as a society are more kind to children, and take their needs more seriously, than Victorian and pre-industrial societies did; that education frees us from poverty and enslavement; that it will enable us to trade and collaborate with other nations. Extended into the realm of religious education, cultural capital might also be buying for us a shared belief that we are becoming more tolerant and reasonable than our forbears.

These beliefs – all of them comfortable, none falsifiable, most unconsciously held – are taken as self-evident, and they exert a huge but largely unexamined influence on the actions and thoughts of individuals in a society, for example by creating conditions in which the large majority of parents assume that schooling is a necessary good for their child.[7]

In a system of free compulsory universal education – a phrase compiled with unconscious irony – the compulsory has become more important than the free. The result is that we are offering, too often, an object that we think a privilege to young people who doubt its usefulness, let alone its specialness.

The pupils' voices at the top of this chapter express vividly their concern about the lack of relevance their schooling had to issues that will face them after school, particularly the threat of economic collapse and ecological breakdown. Some of the students were enabled to experience a different way of learning, in which inter-disciplinary approaches were co-designed by adults and students, all learning together to address a real-world issue with an approach led by questions. Having experienced this, one 14-year-old remarked on the contrast with his own schooling: 'there was no "I will give you this information and you will absorb it."'

Official discourses about why we send young people to school are available. In the United States, no national statement of aims exists, but the federal No Child Left Behind Act of 2001, which continues to be highly influential on all schools and the curricula from kindergarten to Grade 12 in all states, set out its strategic purpose as 'to ensure that all children have a fair, equal, and significant opportunity to obtain a high-quality education'.[8]

While evidently a noble and attractive cultural norm, this masks a circular argument: the purpose of the education system is to make sure that all children have access to the education system. Likewise, the equivalent purposes of schooling in the UK are stated in the terms of their strategic usefulness to the education system, and the body politic as a whole, rather than their direct impact on children as learners. The purposes are to establish an entitlement, to establish national standards, promote continuity and coherence, and promote public understanding.[9]

The aims of schooling in England, and the aims of the curriculum, were stated in 1988 in terms that are static and abstract:

> The school curriculum should aim to provide opportunities for all pupils to learn and to achieve;
> The school curriculum should aim to promote pupils' spiritual, moral, social and cultural development, and prepare pupils for the opportunities, responsibilities and experiences of life.[10]

The 2007 secondary curriculum, and the proposed 2010 primary curriculum, used aims that addressed more directly the question of what pupils should become, with reference to the Every Child Matters outcomes. These aims have apparently been adopted by the coalition government as aims for the whole national curriculum, both primary and secondary, according to which it should enable all young people to become:

- successful learners who enjoy learning, make progress and achieve;
- confident individuals who are able to live safe, healthy and fulfilling lives;
- responsible citizens who make a positive contribution to society.

These aims should inform all aspects of teaching and learning and be the starting point for curriculum design.[11]

We see in these recent articulations of purposes and aims a sense that the curriculum should be addressing the learner directly and that the education system should be responsive and transparent to wider society, including the parents and employers who are its users.

In practice, however, neither the 1988 set of aims nor its 2007 successor, nor the statement of purposes, have had any significant penetration into the everyday discourse and thinking of most schools. There, in the offices of curriculum managers, in the subject departmental bases, on training days and in the classrooms, the focus of those strategic purposes and aims is lost in a detailed concern with delivery. Teachers have tended to occupy themselves, sometimes anxiously, with coverage of content, delivery of policy priorities and meeting required national standards. Indeed, there is widespread concern amongst researchers and some school leaders that so many teachers seem to understand their role in terms of 'delivery', and there is an aspiration to see them more as proactive designers of curriculum aims, content and pedagogy within a loose national parameter. Behind the chosen delivery focus is a conscious or unconscious assumption that the strategic purposes and aims must be someone else's concern – that the reasons why we have schools are obvious, and do not need to be discussed, or at least not today, not here and now.

In the official statements, the use of the word 'entitlement' is significant, and might be a clue to how schools came to be so silent on their purposes. The children's right to a free universal education has been enacted, in most democratic states, as the state's obligation to provide schools, the schools' obligation to provide prescribed educational experiences, and the parents' obligation to send their children to school (or to provide at home an education whose quality and standards are defined by the state). The entitlement of the child to a broad, balanced and coherent curriculum and appropriate standards has been enshrined in England through legal measures such as the 1988 Education Reform Act;[12] the urge to guarantee that entitlement, to deliver on its promise, has been a motivating factor in the standards agenda as expressed through para-legal instruments such as the national strategies.[13] These measures began life as a public commitment to an entitlement: specifically, to raising standards and making success accessible for all learners. But they have produced a superstructure of approved content, levels of attainment, investment in resources, official definitions of good practice and forms of prescriptiveness with regard to pedagogies. Notionally this superstructure exists to improve the performance of schools and the life chances of pupils. However, it has had a distorting effect. Many teachers, as reported in Robin Alexander's review of primary education, feel that the promise of a broad, balanced and rich curriculum has been sacrificed to the standards agenda, and that the curriculum, having started as a 'dream at conception', has become a 'nightmare at delivery'.[14] School improvement and the standards agenda have created a discourse – driving up standards, setting targets, relentless focus on achievement, roll-outs, sectors, cohorts, compliance – which tends to be implicitly mechanistic,[15] and has therefore fostered a factory model of education. It has created an education business in which nearly all teachers and some policy makers feel that the levels of prescriptiveness are unreasonably and unproductively high.

Leading voices in the new coalition government have pointed this out and vowed to sweep away much of the superstructure, for example removing several statutory duties, reviewing all non-statutory guidance and restoring academic freedoms to teachers.[16] How much of this rhetoric will become reality remains to be seen. Meanwhile, we must question any system that begins with a discourse of empowerment, offering education as a liberation from poverty, and which arrives, at this point in history, at a discourse of obligation on schools and parents, and compulsion on teachers and children. The compliance culture in schools remains very strong, and has not yet been much diluted by the government's reforms. Indeed, according to one experienced educator, the powers of successive Secretaries of State for Education have increased from three in 1944, to 250 in 1988, to 2,000 at present,[17] with an estimated 50 more as the result of current legislation.[18] In addition to those legal powers, their ability to invest money in approved projects means that they have 'tasted the heady brew of backing their pet ideas with money'.[19] The contradiction between a rhetoric of liberation and a reality of compulsion has reached its sharpest point so far in the Secretary of State's drive to force some primary and secondary schools into academy status. Head teachers have, in their own words, been 'told to make a choice' for academy status, which parents in some of the affected schools feel is 'dogmatic', 'dictatorial' and 'treating them with contempt'.[20]

The long-term accretion of centralized power, often accompanied by a rhetoric of trusting teachers and devolving to local structures, is seen by some leading educational researchers as being anti-democratic and in urgent need of reversal.[21] Since the birth of the coalition government, centralized educational power has grown stronger, for example through prescriptive curriculum measures such as the English Baccalaureate[22] and the insistence on only one prime approach to teaching reading.[23]

We are faced with an initial contradiction that the original intention to provide educational opportunities for all, including an aspiration to offer religious education for the spiritual development of pupils and society, has become enmeshed in a corporate-state model in which the dominant ethic is composed of legal compulsion, and hegemonic and random notions of good practice and professional delivery. Entitlement has mutated into enforcement, and this has serious consequences for the way in which teachers and learners see religious education.

Which school shall I go to, what choice do I have and how much does my choice matter?

Rising levels of poverty, inequality and fear make all choices about the public provision of schooling politically edged. Decisions affect not only the share of financial resources but also the definitions of the frontiers of state, voluntary and private responsibility:

> What services must have cast-iron guarantees of nationwide standards, parity and continuity? ... How, therefore, does national government underwrite these strategic 'absolutes'? ... What is too important to be left to even the most resourceful localism?[24]

Thus the Archbishop of Canterbury poses the questions to which, he argues, government has so far avoided giving answers; a government that, in the midst of a financial crisis that is ruining whole communities, appears not yet to have realized how destabilizing and frightening these circumstances have become for many.

Western education systems must now be concerned with the extent to which a national education system can be responsive to the needs of the children, families and communities that use it, and the priorities placed on it by policy makers. The interplay between local responsiveness and national policy has become highly conflicted in some national systems. In the English system until the 1980s, there was a pure belief that local authorities held the ring, disbursing educational resources accountably and being answerable to parents through local elections. Most publicly maintained schools were comprehensive, most parents sent their child to the local school. Schooling, it was therefore believed, could be responsive to need, while policy priorities could be resourced according to the processes of democratic politics. By this arrangement, social inequalities were at least held stable, and some social justice objectives could be achieved.[25]

But that arrangement was far from perfect. It began to break down because of the persistence of selective schools, and is now disintegrating under wave on wave of new types of schools with diverse accountabilities: grant-maintained schools, city technology colleges, old academies, new academies, trust schools and free schools. All of these different categories of school have their own legally defined relationship with the state and the curriculum, whether by law or contract. The insertion of more parental choice into this equation has had far-reaching consequences, among which, for example, is the reality that the many different types of school are not all equally regarded. External measurements and league tables influence the media and therefore parental opinion. Faith communities are playing an increasing role as providers of schools. According to Tim Brighouse, the 'mantra' of choice and diversity has grown to have a damaging effect on equality of opportunity over the last 30 years.[26]

Parents are both players and pawns in this. Egged on by legislation and exhortation, they can become key players, triggering legislation or getting their own way in local school admissions and curriculum issues.[27] Yet legislation to prioritize parental choice in schooling has resulted in schools being able to select parents, and this has led to greater inequalities, something acknowledged by conservative minister David Willettts.[28] Marketization of schools has accelerated under the coalition government, with many schools – ultimately, most if not all – transferring to academy status, outside the frame of local government, less accountable to communities or families. The combined impact of deregulation and public sector cutbacks has sacrificed many services for the poorest, such as support for special needs and emotional and behavioural difficulties, as well as severely reducing the advisory services that support teachers. Increasingly, local authorities, schools and academies are finding that they cannot afford to provide some services, are no longer legally obliged to do so, or will not be inspected on them. By a combination of design and accident, many of the provisions that held inequality in check, however inadequately, are fast disappearing. It is now predicted that within a short number of years, there will be no viable local authority system of accountability for schools, and no clear alternative to take its place.[29] In this radical rearrangement of structures, Mel Ainscow, an educationalist with expertise in equality measures, predicts that the policy of marketization and deregulation will create winners and losers.[30] The corporate winners are the sponsors of new academies, the elite universities and the children who gain entry to them. In the background of this straightforwardly conservative programme, it has been startling to hear the mood music of the Secretary of State's moral outrage against inequality in education. He has called for schools to be 'engines of social mobility, helping children to overcome the accidents of birth and background'.[31] We see the 'swift but steady transfer of resources from the needy to the better off, in the name of the disadvantaged'.[32] The advantaged enclaves sometimes include faith communities, which have been encouraged to establish academies and free schools, and thus have a contributing interest in the direction of structural change.

Some politicians in positions of responsibility for education have announced their commitment to working with teachers to raise standards, and their preference for leaving structures unchanged or giving away power. Some feel queasy about imposing structural change; Stephen Twigg, Labour's Shadow Secretary of State for Education, confesses that 'in government, [we] emphasized structures a bit too much.'[33] Others, such as Estelle Morris, have accepted that standards and structures are inter-dependent, so that influencing the former requires some changes to the latter, but she applies the question of whether the political option of changing structures to allow more choice and diversity is the only or most effective lever on standards.[34] The current coalition government's programme is premised on profound structural change, convinced that this alone will deliver the looked-for rise in standards:

> We will promote the reform of schools in order to ensure that new providers can enter the state school system ... [and] that all schools have greater freedom over the curriculum ... we will give parents, teachers, charities and local communities the chance to set up new schools.[35]

This programme is seen by the coalition as part of a larger canvas of structural change, sometimes known as the 'tight/loose balance'. Outlined by the government's big society thinker Francis Maude, this canvas envisages frontline work done by or on behalf of government being given more operational responsibility while at the same time having tighter controls, greater efficiency and quality expectations.[36] Yet what does this mean for parents, communities, children and their teachers? We may have to search further than this idea for any coherent answer to the Archbishop of Canterbury's questions.

Thus our second contradiction is that an education system, including religious education offered to all, moves suddenly from a compliance culture to a marketized and deregulated state, but with key elements even more centralized, creating near chaos. Successive politicians, announcing their concern for standards, end up changing structures. Religious education, having survived on the strength of its statutory position, sees its structural support being progressively whittled away. A subject in need of benefiting from new structures is caught in the collapsing rubble of the old. A subject that aims to deepen young people's care and concern for those who are different or vulnerable finds that it has to defend its existence in a hostile or indifferent world.

What should I be taught in school?

If the questions of why and where I go to school are explicitly political, and the answers on offer highly conflicted, the issue of what should be in the school curriculum is more implicitly so – no less problematic, but perhaps less obviously so.

The question of whether there should be a national curriculum at all has been disputed in some jurisdictions. In the United States, the No Child Left Behind Act of 2001, together with subsequent measures to define minimum standards and core entitlements for all learners, excited much critical comment, but remains a key policy of a Secretary for Education who believes in its capacity to raise standards and close the rich–poor gap.[37] However, some leading educationalists have questioned its effectiveness in those objectives, and denounced its prescriptiveness.[38] In England, the legislation to introduce a full-scale national curriculum in 1988 was controversial. Since then, arguments about its right to exist have long lain dormant, but are now alive again. The UK parliament's Select Committee dealing with schools and education raised challenges to the curriculum's existence and its proposed levels of prescriptiveness in 2010. After taking evidence and considerable internal discussion, its support for a continued national curriculum was lukewarm at its strongest, and hedged with conditions. It called for a national curriculum

> underpinned by the principle that it should seek to prescribe as little as possible and by the principle of subsidiarity, with decisions made at the lowest appropriate level.[39]

With the multiplying curriculum variations ushered in by greater curriculum freedom comes a question: do we need a national curriculum at all? Keri Facer argues that the notion of a national curriculum is essentially a twentieth-century central-planning model that lacks the capacity to enable teachers and young people to deal creatively with the unpredictabilities of the twenty-first century. This, Facer argues, is because it is premised on long-term modelling, is too statist to deliver social justice or equality, and blanks out children's own knowledge and experience.[40] Michael Young argues that the case for a national curriculum is not so much political as epistemological, since it defines the knowledge that we intend to convey[41] – a point made repeatedly by Mick Waters when leading the curriculum division of the now defunct Qualifications and Curriculum Authority.

The probable intention behind conceptualizing a curriculum as the knowledge, understanding and skills that we as a nation choose to put before our young people is to introduce, however vaguely, a sense of shared ownership. It leaves many questions unanswered: who are we as a nation, how do we make our curriculum opinions heard, why nation and not local area? If 'we as a nation' works for us, are we content that it should work equally for national contexts where secular or theocratic dictatorships determine the knowledge base? What account should we take of global factors – conflict, debt, environmental collapse, energy and water shortages, in shaping our knowledge? Nevertheless, the proposal that national communities can and should have a sense of mutual responsibility in shaping and presenting learning is a reasonable one, flexible enough to be the framework for many different versions of a national curriculum.

Since the 1988 Education Reform Act, the evolutions of the curriculum have moved it from a model of prescribed knowledge through a conventional range of subjects, towards more complex, though less lengthy versions that emphasized social ends and means. At the time of writing it seems possible that the original model of curriculum as syllabus of knowledge may be reinstated.

At each key stage of compulsory education, up to age 16, the national curriculum provided programmes of study for the 'core' subjects of English, mathematics and science and the 'foundation subjects' of art, geography, history, music, physical education and technology, later adding modern foreign languages from age 11 and, later still, citizenship. Schools were also required to teach religious education, though this subject sat outside the National Curriculum itself.[42] Religious education had national documents,[43] shadowing the wider curriculum's aims and structure, in 1994, 2004, 2007 and 2010: these documents were not statutory, but they had wide influence on local curriculum planning in RE. In subsequent curriculum reviews, a number of non-statutory subjects such as personal, social and health education, and 'cross-curricular' themes and skills, were added to this basic framework in the course of implementation.

In response to teachers' complaints that the National Curriculum and its testing arrangements were too unwieldy, the Dearing Review of 1993 slimmed down the content of programmes of study, and introduced generic-level descriptions, defining pupil attainment on an eight-level scale for each subject for the first time. Subsequent reviews in 1999 and 2007 enacted further reductions in prescribed content, and introduced an overt statement of aims, values and purposes.[44]

The 2007 review of the secondary curriculum, and the 2009–10 proposals for a primary curriculum, paid closer attention to curriculum design as a way of helping schools to use their freedom and flexibility to best effect, while also embedding key contemporary government priorities such as narrowing the rich–poor attainment gap, Every Child Matters and financial capability.

Historically, the curriculum has not always been considered as a means to strategic goals such as raising standards, improving schools or closing the gap. It had perhaps been more common for schools to seek other avenues for addressing those issues, such as behaviour management, teaching and learning approaches and staff accountability. Yet Ofsted's research report, 'Twelve Outstanding Secondary Schools',[45] showed how the curriculum could be either a strategic aid or an impediment to strategic goals.

Curriculum design is a political issue because it influences pedagogy, and therefore the progress of pupils, in invisible ways. Public pressure groups often exert influence to have their cause included in the content of the curriculum, be it an aspect of child safety, an approach to language teaching, an outdoor experience or a particular skill or value. This applies as much with religious and belief communities, who are actively seeking ways to ensure that their belief is included in official documents at local and national level. Curriculum writers can only agree at the cost of having very lengthy documents, considered too prescriptive. On the other hand, reducing content to a bare minimum incurs the disappointment of many pressure groups and may lead to their cause disappearing from some or most schools.

Behind this conundrum, however, lies a misconception: namely that enforcing content will in itself address an issue. For example, if the teaching of healthy cooking and eating is made statutory, will this reduce obesity? Does statutory coverage of principal religions lead to better community relations? It would hardly be possible to devise a controlled research project that yielded a reliable answer. Yet the causal link is often assumed, by pressure groups and teachers. This leads to a fragmentary approach to curriculum design, in which the details of content are built up without a sense of the overall coherence or purpose, like a piece-by-piece mosaic with no overall picture.

Designing a curriculum around knowledge alone tends to produce 'delivery' teachers whose pedagogical default style is invariant content coverage. It takes a rare teacher to transform such a curriculum – which is really a syllabus – into learning experiences that absorb the learner and vivify the subject. This is as difficult as turning flat cola into sparkling champagne. Content-led teaching favours teachers and learners in privileged environments, where less skill and effort are required to interest and motivate learners. Correspondingly, in more challenging schools a flat, content-led design will either create more planning challenges for teachers, or become a deficit that is passed on to the learners, whose progress suffers as a result. In RE, it has long been known that a content-led approach simply induces boredom, apathy or hostility; distressingly however, many local RE syllabuses, and therefore many lessons and units, repeat this pattern.[46]

Alternative designs have offered aims-led, concept-led or experience-led models of curriculum planning, which leave decisions on detailed content, beyond what is illustrated, to schools operating in their local communities. Key concepts can be understood as major, archetypal ideas that exist in each subject and can be linked to several different forms of content.

Each successive curriculum review has aimed at generating a less prescriptive and less content-led model, yet has attempted to do more to embed overarching moral, social and economic goals. There remains a question as to whether the embedding of such goals has helped educators or has distorted the system within which they work: some, such as Neil Postman, have argued that social and economic goals, and the fragmentary priorities that derive from them, have robbed education of any transcending narrative of personal meaning for teachers and young people.[47] In England, successive curriculum reviews have tended to be conducted in complete isolation from qualification development and pedagogy, thus giving the system a fragmentary and incoherent nature. The complexity of curriculum structure, lack of coherence with other elements of the education system, and excessively burdensome superstructures have been the key perceived weaknesses of the model that pertained up until 2010.

This evolutionary project has now been abandoned by the coalition government, intent on reducing the curriculum to a traditional, narrow core of knowledge, and interested in curriculum design only in so far as it guarantees coherence and sets schools free.[48]

Proposing a curriculum composed of core knowledge, in which a traditional range of subjects act independently of each other, raises a number of political questions. What is the core knowledge of a discipline? Does it ever change? Can the state itemize this knowledge without relapsing into excessive prescriptiveness? What would RE look like if it were defined by knowledge alone?[49] How does knowledge get used, how can it transform the prospects of poorer individuals or communities? How will schools be expected to build beyond knowledge to embrace understanding, skills, dispositions and experiences? If they are left to define their own way in this, what will be the safeguards against inappropriate models becoming dominant, perhaps because they are cheap or simple?

Conclusion

The question now facing developed education systems is stark: in an era of diminishing resources and widening inequalities, how can schooling systems ensure universal rights and standards, while also avoiding statist solutions? How can they promote educational liberty, creativity and innovation, while also ensuring strategic approaches to breaking the link between child poverty and underperformance? Perhaps this cannot be done: perhaps electorates and parents must choose between a system engineered for creativity, with excellent elites, or one catering for equality, with limits on freedom.

We continue to pay for a public system of compulsory education, including RE, because of vague, unexamined yet tenacious beliefs that it cures a scarcity or offers cultural capital. Nationally and locally, we have not sat down and had out what we want, distinguishing that which can reasonably be obtained from that which is unrealistic. A growing sense of crisis, including a crisis of expectations and scepticism about value for money, lingers in the education system, making it more vulnerable to critiques from small-government conservatives. For example, Frank Furedi's angry call for the educational superstructure of child psychologists, advisers, trainers, behaviour specialists to be swept away, along with the advice and guidance they proffer,[50] has clearly found a willing audience amongst coalition government ministers. The argument that the curriculum and pedagogy superstructure had become too complex and prescriptive, and needed to be stripped back to a core; the belief that making space for creativity and local responsiveness will also narrow the achievement gap for the poorest – these unproven assumptions have started to take root and, by *force majeure*, will become the dominant doxa or beliefs of the next few years, concentrating cultural capital in the hands of those who already have its economic equivalent. The proffered solutions of freedom are questionable, but may be proved right in time: whether they are wrong or right, teachers will try to make them work, and policy makers will claim they work better.

In this future, religious education might or might not survive. Its capacity to do so will depend not on any almighty legal or para-legal prescriptions, and not on the advocacy of religious groups alone, but on its evolutionary adaptation to a much more challenging educational climate: unequal, diversified, demand-led, randomly combining local distinctiveness with central diktat, sporadically innovative, permanently changing. In the next chapter, RE's fitness to face these challenges is critically examined, specifically in relation to pedagogy.

Response from Clive Erricker

The importance of Mark's chapter is that he takes us back to uncover what the prime purposes of education might be and whether schools and the school curriculum are sufficient vehicles, as they stand, to deliver on those purposes. As with much of the thinking and practice we analyse in this book, there seems to be an avoidance of deep questioning concerning what education should really be about and in what ways it rests on a vision for society and its values. This in turn impacts on RE itself as one component of the education project.

The contradiction Mark highlights between entitlement which then mutates into enforcement and obligation is indicative of the Kafkaesque bewilderment and catch-22 logic that we encounter repeatedly. The tensions between centrally stated outcomes as a marker of success (GCSE passes in the

English Baccalaureate) and the desire to deregulate the educational model by seeking willing providers is another example of avoiding thinking through the ultimate educational goals and the social purposes they are founded upon. This has nothing to do with seeking to ensure a just and equal democratic society and everything to do with deregulating whilst maintaining control.

It is not fanciful to compare this situation with what is happening in the financial sector, as referred to in Chapter 1. Whereas banks and financial institutions remain fully unregulated despite their calamitous contribution to the parlous state of the world economy and the nation's wealth, schools are viewed as ongoing disaster areas that never sufficiently deliver due to their past regulation. So, make them more like banks, just make sure, in crude terms, that they know what they have to deliver, in a material sense. This is the way of hyper-capitalist democracies. Forget attention to overall social purposes, just offer the ephemeral notion of freedom and we can hope for the best outcome. Education is no exception to this. To balance the argument, regulation is not a panacea. The answer lies in the attempt to fully engage with what education is for and whether schools can provide the means to ensure that the purposes of education are met.

Part 2

Diagnosing RE's pedagogy, provenance and politics

Chapter 3

The heart of the enterprise
A pedagogical problem

Mark Chater

Opening story

Year 8 (mainly 12-year-olds) in a local community school have RE with Mrs Robinson. They are well-behaved, dutiful learners, not the most imaginative or sparky, but well disposed and well prepared to learn in lessons. They quite like RE and they know Mrs Robinson, having had her for RE last year. It is near the start of a new term, and Mrs Robinson has been on a professional development course about 'learning from' religion and belief – the second of the two attainment targets in her local agreed syllabus. As a result of this, she wants to try some different approaches to RE.

The unit they are doing is about Christianity – exploring its core beliefs about Jesus and its impact on believers today. In one lesson, they examine St Mark's Gospel for sources of the Christian belief that Jesus was the son of God. They look at the story of Jesus calming the storm, paying particular attention to the verse, 'who is this man, that even the wind and the waves obey him?' She explains to the class how people believed that being the son of God would include having power over nature, so any story about Jesus showing this power was intended to be a sign of his being the son of God, the Christ.

Like many teachers, Mrs Robinson has devised aims for this lesson. In this case, she has one 'learning about' aim, and one 'learning from'. She considers this an appropriate, balanced approach to planning. For 'learning about', the aim is that pupils will be able to explain the intended meaning behind the story of Jesus calming the waves. For 'learning from', it is that pupils will respond to the story by reflecting on the storms in their own lives.

After ensuring that pupils have met the first aim by writing down, in their own words, why the Gospel writer told stories about Jesus and his power over nature, she led them on to the second aim. She asked them to draw a picture of Jesus, the boat, the disciples and the stormy sea, and place themselves in the picture. 'What are the storms that frighten you in your life?' she asks. 'What things worry you most, and how would you like someone to calm them down?' She is careful not to indoctrinate them into assuming that the 'someone' must necessarily be Jesus.

The pupils are puzzled. 'Miss, do you mean, like, real storms, tornadoes and stuff?' 'I've seen a tornado.' 'Did you see that twister programme?' Once she has them re-focused, she explains that she meant inner storms. A few pupils understand this, and rise to the challenge thoughtfully. Mrs Robinson closes the lesson by asking them all to be still and think how grateful they are to have a friend who can calm their storms in times of trouble.

The pupils leave in good order, and Mrs Robinson is pleased. But most of them have not been able to see the connection between the first and second parts of the lesson. The following week she sees them again for RE. At the start of the lesson, when she questions them, some say the previous lesson had been a story about Jesus, while others say it was about being grateful for friends.

Introduction

RE teachers may well disagree about the worthwhileness of the lesson described in this story. Some might like it as an example of making RE relevant to the learners. Others might be mildly concerned about the chosen method for doing so – perhaps worrying about the potential intrusion on pupils' inner lives. Others still might be profoundly critical of the lesson's basic structure and the relationship, or lack of it, between learning about and learning from. Before reading any further, you might wish to pause and decide on your opinion of the lesson.

Why did Mrs Robinson choose to plan in this way? We assume that her professional development course encouraged her to be more adventurous in promoting 'learning from', which is often seen as the poor relation of the two RE attainment targets. She sees the logic that RE must have personal relevance in order to be compelling and alive as learning. We do not know whether or not she was specifically advised to plan with two aims, one for learning about and one for learning from. The selection of content – Jesus calming the storm – would probably have been determined by a departmental scheme of work or the local syllabus. The choice of 'inner storms' as a theme for the second half of the lesson, matching 'learning from', was perhaps hers alone, reflecting her intuitive response to the story. We cannot know for certain what influenced her to structure the lesson in that way.

It is the argument of this chapter that Mrs Robinson's planning approach is quite widespread in RE, and that it reveals the profoundest lack of teacher understanding of the subject – a deficit which is wreaking long-term damage on RE's credibility with pupils and colleagues alike. It is clear that Mrs

Robinson is well-intentioned: caring towards her pupils, willing to innovate, scrupulous to avoid straying into a Christian nurture method. In these qualities, Mrs Robinson is like many other primary and secondary teachers of RE. It is probable that the example narrated above, and others like it in real classrooms, have not in themselves damaged pupils in any serious way. Why, then, should we be concerned and critical? First, because Mrs Robinson has not decided whether she is teaching about Christian beliefs or personal well-being; next, her lesson attempts vainly to bridge this gulf and, as a result, fails to be coherent for most learners; third, because a repeated diet of such lessons – planned schizophrenically – will, in the medium term, undermine pupils' progress in RE, compromising the strength of their understanding of Christianity and introducing distractors, like an array of bright fruit snatched in passing from other branches; fourth, because her commitment to making RE relevant is based on a fear that it is not: that, in this example, the sources of Christian belief about Jesus as Messiah might not be sufficiently interesting in themselves. The question then arises: why compel learners to work with this content, if one fears that it has no direct relevance to them? There are many good and honest answers to that, within the parameters of a community school in which no particular faith is identified with the school ethos. The answers might be to change the content; or to teach it because of this country's Christian history and culture; or to teach it because it is pure knowledge; or to teach it with personal relevance, but find some other way of bridging the relevance gulf.

Such as? Mrs Robinson wishes to improve her lessons, but is now a little resentful that her ideas and practice have been criticized. One way to introduce personal relevance into a lesson on St Mark's claim that Jesus was the Christ is simply to ask pupils whether they agree. This may seem like a high-risk strategy, guaranteed to offend Christian parents and others equally; it may seem too uncomfortably similar to old-fashioned confessional approaches. But these dangers can be navigated with some common-sense safeguards based on rules of discussion. The pupils would now know that they have a real opportunity to learn from the idea of Jesus as Messiah, by reflecting on it, perhaps particularly reflecting on whether they would be convinced if they personally saw someone who could make the wind and waves obey him. They would find that their teacher's invitation to reflect and respond is about something recognizably the same as the earlier part of the lesson. They would overcome their confusion as to what the lesson was truly 'about'. They would be more ready to take the next step. They would find, in time, that their power to reflect and respond deepens, becomes more nuanced, more aware of diverse and complex answers, as they listen to each other and notice how their own views have changed. They would be making progress in learning about and from.

Why is it that so few teachers of RE engage with this train of thought? Why is it that Ofsted[1] observes so many lessons in which the learning is designed in a muddled way? This is a problem of pedagogy, but it is not confined to classroom methodology. The problem is distributed widely throughout the entire range of RE documentation and thinking, both at official levels and in theoretical constructs of RE.

RE's pedagogical problem

Pedagogy, which can roughly mean the process by which the child is led to learning, is a complex set of forces acting on every teacher, whether they know it or not. These forces include the curriculum but also the surrounding culture and the lifeworlds of the children – and above all, the depth of the teacher's own understanding of all these. While there will be many who define pedagogy simply in terms of the methods chosen for teaching in the classroom, there is a more complex and rewarding sense of the word, in which the ideas of the curriculum, the ideas, theories and values in the surrounding culture, and the quality of the teacher's grasp of these items, all converge in the classroom and impact on the quality of planning and teaching.[2]

In many European contexts, university courses to prepare teachers have honoured this complexity by bringing together, under the heading of pedagogy, a general humanist studies approach encompassing philosophy, ethics, psychology and child development, amongst other disciplines. These perspectives lead up to instruction in methods, and they inform the choices that are made in selecting content.[3] In the UK and United States, the tendency has been to divorce pedagogy from curriculum content in a dualism of 'how' and 'what'. Thus, for example, the remits given to national educational agencies in the UK made it clear that the government believed it had a legal duty to determine curriculum content (through a curriculum agency) and to set standards for examinations (through a qualifications watchdog). To a lesser extent, not set in legislation, the government also insisted on specific learning and teaching approaches (through its national strategies). The distinction between a curriculum remit and a pedagogy remit was vigilantly maintained by government and opposition politicians; any perceived infringements were criticized.

This leads us on to our present state of affairs. The distinction that governments can legislate on curriculum, but not pedagogy, forms a central assumption on the part of the current Secretary of State for Education, Michael Gove. Announcing his intention to scale back state prescriptiveness, as part of a strategy to set head teachers free from central control, he described the notion of curriculum in terms of 'facts' and said that teaching methods should be left entirely to teachers: 'I just think there should be facts.'[4] Having applied this what/how dualism, and clearly believing its attractive simplicity, Mr Gove is then able to define the curriculum as 'knowledge' and pedagogy as 'method'. Many would applaud this as a policy position.

But a powerful and dangerous reduction is at work. In order to accept that there can be an absolute distinction between the state's control over the content of the curriculum and the teacher's choice of teaching methods, we must abandon as too complex the conception of the curriculum as a set of aims, ideas and skills, all working coherently to promote particular pedagogical stances; we must also jettison the notion that pedagogy is a sophisticated understanding of one's subject, its place in culture and history, its relationship to other subjects, its rules of engagement with children. Such definitions are airily dismissed as unnecessary guidance or impractical theorizing. The idea that curriculum and pedagogy might be related to each other, and might influence each other for good or ill, is well grounded in research on effective learning. Traditional, teacher-dominated approaches tend to inhibit classroom life unless interventions, such as transformative curriculum models, are there to counter them.[5] But this body of theory is swept away by the curriculum/pedagogy dualism and the logic emergent from it. The pursuit of this logic leads us back to Mrs Robinson, a teacher whose choice of classroom methods is severed from any thinking about the nature and purpose of the subject, its place in the curriculum and its dealings with wider society.[6]

An alternative notion, offered by Robin Alexander, is that pedagogy forms the 'attendant discourse' informing and justifying both curriculum selection and classroom method.[7] In this notion, pedagogy is prior to curriculum and method; a teacher's pedagogical understanding is not individuated and isolated, but is part of a communal understanding of why they are teaching a subject – an understanding contextualized in a department, school, community, professional association or network. A shared pedagogical understanding can be a culturally rich bed in which different types of practitioner knowledge flower. From Jerome Bruner we learn that if the shared understanding is critical and dynamic, not composed of received wisdom, folk wisdom or rigid traditionalism, it will be so much the stronger in allowing teachers to apply their insights to the aims of their work.[8] From John Dewey we take the belief that a teacher's knowledge of social conditions, and understanding of civilization, are necessary in order to interpret what they do with the learner.[9] From contemporary essays on pedagogical thinking we can note a particular concern that its scope should include values and beliefs as well as strategies and techniques.[10] It is this wide scope to pedagogy, at once complex and contested, which attracts some teachers and repels many. As a way of understanding and positioning pedagogy, this helps RE because there is a constant need to be clear about why we are teaching it, in what context and with what definitions of success.

The attendant discourse identifiable for RE must, of necessity, be carefully mapped by everyone preparing to teach it, given the sensitivity of people's cherished beliefs and the profound life questions explored. A very brief itemization of the probable attendant discourse would include popular and scholarly perceptions of the place and impact of religion, and of non-religious worldviews, in local, national and global life. It would rehearse the ways by which different branches of RE – historical, literary, sociological, ethical – are studied: for example, it would ensure teachers understand the nature of myth in religious studies, employing a range of critical hermeneutic tools and perhaps comparing those tools with the related, but different implements used in history and literature. In this way it would be clear about the intellectual rules of engagement that apply in RE. Perhaps most important, the attendant discourse would require of teachers that they have examined the layered development of different rationales for RE – cultural, confessional, phenomenological, experiential, conceptual – that exist in the UK, and reached some settled, though still evolving, position for themselves, so that they have a clear answer when a colleague asks: 'Why are you teaching RE?' or when a pupil asks: 'Why do we have to learn this?'

The avoidance of these attendant discourses for RE, in initial and continuing development of teachers that are too rushed to address such complexity, has damaged the credibility of RE. Like a hole below the water line, this hidden infringement has let in a heavy mass of confused practice which might, in time, capsize the subject.

In this chapter, pedagogy is taken to mean much more than method: it is a complex set of cultural forces acting on the teacher. Pedagogical knowledge in RE has a meaning that goes far beyond technical knowledge of how to teach: it means a reflective journey, with some worked-out awareness of the place of religion and belief and its impact on the modern world, including the teacher's own feelings and opinions on it; following from this, a reason or set of reasons to teach RE, and a clear sense of the delineations of the subject – what it can and cannot achieve, what it should and should not attempt – from this flows an informed and sensitive selection of content; and from this, coupled with knowledge of the pupils and the community, come decisions on how to construct the learning and build individual lessons. The planning of individual lessons is the tip of the iceberg, the only part visible to learners, senior leaders and inspectors; yet it cannot survive without the mass of thought that lies under the surface. Teachers of other subjects must undergo similar trains of thought, but in the case of RE, the profile of religion and the sensitivity accompanying the ways in which people commit to it, stay in it or reject it are such that greater than normal care must be taken in pedagogy. RE's pedagogical problem is essentially a problem of its message to the learner and the outside world, its identity as a subject. It is, in Alexander's phrase, 'the heart of the enterprise',[11] the place we must start if we are to understand how to improve RE. Pedagogy starts with the ways of understanding the subject's overall purpose and rationale, and feeds through into syllabus design and planning:

> it gives life to educational aims and values, lifts the curriculum from the printed page, mediates learning and knowing, engages, inspires and empowers learners – or, sadly, may fail to do so.[12]

Pedagogical models that are ill thought through, or slightly dishonest, will sometimes result in avoidance of difficult questions from pupils, 'happy ending' lessons which promote only the positive facets of religion, or simplistic frameworks of understanding imposed on complex systems of thought. This in turn produces, too often, an incomplete or poor pupil understanding, even of the dominant religion, Christianity.[13] It can also trigger feelings of pupil discomfort or embarrassment in relation to RE.

There are pedagogical lessons in pupil discomfort. Given any opportunity, 'pupils will soon ask the unanswerable questions.'[14] It is the task of competent RE teachers, whether primary or secondary, to draw on their own rich, evolving pedagogical knowledge in response.

Pedagogy and purpose

The construction of pedagogical knowledge for RE should begin with an understanding of religion, belief and education. This book has already offered an argument on the place of religion and belief in the modern world (Chapter 1), and the conflicted state of education (Chapter 2). So we should next examine the question of RE's rationale, something often side-stepped by teachers anxious to develop practical ideas. But in order to plan and teach RE well, it is absolutely necessary for teachers to understand why they are doing it – not just the aims for a lesson, not even the overall aims of the subject, but its rationale: the argument it 'puts up' for laying a claim to compulsory curriculum time. In England, the commonest version of this rationale is in the national framework for RE, a document that was first published in 2004, and revised to fit into new curriculum proposals in 2007–8 and 2009–10. In its original form, it says this:

> Religious education provokes challenging questions about the ultimate meaning and purpose of life, beliefs about God, the self and the nature of reality, issues of right and wrong and what it means to be human. It develops pupils' knowledge and understanding of Christianity, other principal religions, other religious traditions and other world views that offer answers to questions such as these. It offers opportunities for personal reflection and spiritual development. It enhances pupils' awareness and understanding of religions and beliefs, teachings, practices and forms of expression, as well as of the influence of religion on individuals, families, communities and cultures. Religious education encourages pupils to learn from different religions, beliefs, values and traditions while exploring their own beliefs and questions of meaning. It challenges pupils to reflect on, consider, analyse, interpret and evaluate issues of truth, belief, faith and ethics and to communicate their responses. Religious education encourages pupils to develop their sense of identity and belonging. It enables them to flourish individually within their

communities and as citizens in a pluralistic society and global community. Religious education has an important role in preparing pupils for adult life, employment and lifelong learning. It enables pupils to develop respect for and sensitivity to others, in particular those whose faiths and beliefs are different from their own. It promotes discernment and enables pupils to combat prejudice.[15]

In length and style it is similar to the 'importance statements' of other subjects. This one has influenced, or been copied verbatim into, nearly all local syllabuses, making its arguments very common in the English system. A careful reading of this statement reveals that it was written by a committee. In keeping with the structures and interests of the RE world, it was written with a need to satisfy several communities, whose influence has pulled this statement in many different directions.

The educational voice is heard strongly in the opening phrase: 'RE provokes fundamental questions.' The examples – including mention of what it means to be human, God and right and wrong, bear witness to a need to satisfy both educational and religious lobbies. Significantly, the pursuit of important questions about the human condition is the single strongest element in pupil voices collected by RE's professional association:

What's great about RE is that it provokes challenging questions. ... It is both academic and exploring the depth of human nature.[16]

However, the framework has other themes to add. In the second sentence there is a hierarchy of content: Christianity, other principal religions, other religious traditions and other worldviews – which is clear evidence of a perceived order of importance, whether for cultural or theological reasons. But in a statement on importance and rationale, why get into content at all? Does the content make the importance?

The long sentence in the middle, beginning 'It enhances pupils' awareness' and the next three sentences after it, are essentially a rehearsal of the six strands that compose the content of RE. The long strings of verbs describe, in too much detail for a rationale statement, what is supposed to go in RE, again missing the opportunity to speak about the importance and rationale. Only in the final four sentences, in which it is claimed that RE 'enables [pupils] to flourish individually ... has an important role in preparing pupils for adult life ... enables pupils to develop respect ... promotes discernment' do we find again a voice making claims for our subject – claims of the sort that are clearly intended to speak strongly of the subject's contribution to individuals and society. Yet how verifiable are these claims, and would they be likely to be heard thoughtfully by a doubting parent or head teacher?

In this single statement are the voices of those who argue that RE is an important acknowledgement of our culture, including our recent diversity;

and those who want it to address our religious, cultural and ethnic divisions positively; and those who argue that it is about God, and right and wrong; and those who argue that it promotes values and skills; and those who make a priority of personal reflection and spiritual development; and those educators who say it is the questions, the enquiries, that should drive the subject; and those who would place central value on textual knowledge, understanding, analysis and interpretation; and those who wish to see RE in terms of its instrumental value, for example its impact on employment, community relations or capacity for lifelong learning.

Can it be that one subject is really able to address all these issues as part of its core purpose? It is no criticism of this statement's original authors, nor of the many who have used it or edited it, that it speaks of many purposes: perhaps it does so in order to maintain agreement across the 25 very different signatory organizations, as well as ensuring that the document ticks all the curricular boxes. The statement does a good job of that, and the framework document as a whole is a significant, hard-won and historic achievement. It continues to be politically necessary; but it is also in danger of over-selling RE, confusing or blurring the purposes of the subject, and diluting its strength of purpose through an appeal to too many competing priorities. There are those who would take the critique further, believing that the framework's mixed rationale misrepresents the nature of religion in a misguided campaign to commend RE as contributing to instrumental social aims.[17]

There are many REs, most of them represented in the importance statement. Teachers usually think about the subject with a narrower frame of reference about its purpose. The ancient and new disciplines which are implied in the statement – philosophy, systematic theology, Christian apologetics, sociology, religious studies, biblical studies – form just a few of the constituent disciplines in what is a coalition model of RE. Does this matter? Some other subjects in the school curriculum are also alliances of several disciplines. However, at least two of these – citizenship, design and technology – have been identified and set aside into the basic curriculum.[18] Coalition status can make RE a confusing and confused place, in which there are highly variable rules of engagement, and many different skill sets to develop. This can be handled well, but only if teachers are explicit about what is happening and the skills and attitudes needed to succeed in it. The current importance statement keeps the broad church of the RE community together, fudging its many differences of rationale and blurring together its constituent disciplines. While this has been politically useful, it has also enabled teachers to take the next step – from rationale to planning – largely blind to the confused or undeclared rationale. The hidden confusion is thus passed from top-line statements of principle to classroom-based practice.

The objection can be made that a single rationale for RE might be narrowly restrictive of its possibilities. This chapter does not argue for singleness of purpose, but for clarity and honesty. A teacher may well draw on variable rationales, and distinctive disciplines, and still be effective – if the awareness is there. Alexander speaks of the importance of teacher repertoire,[19] meaning a versatility as to the pedagogical theories and values impacting on the classroom. For example, if a teacher is using a story from a sacred text, is this for purposes of moral development, critical textual study, sourcing of beliefs or something else? The teacher can legitimately announce a change of purpose: 'last week we looked at this story using questions to work out who wrote it and why [adult rationale: a critical approach]. This week we are going to look at the same story but ask what meaning believers take from it, and what meaning we could take from it [adult rationale: a theological approach].' When a teacher signals this versatility to colleagues, parents and learners, the rules of intellectual engagement are clear and the interaction has integrity.

It might also be argued that other subjects have confused rationales and do not seem to suffer from it. Citizenship wants to teach young people to think for themselves, but also to know and value items that can be contested, such as diversity and parliamentary democracy. Other rationales often include a desire to alter the attitudes or behaviour of pupils in ways that, in RE, would be denounced as improper. Musicians want young people to sing and play; PE teachers want pupils to be fit and healthy; and so on. The difficulty here is that RE has hidden its equivalent aspiration for pupils, burying it under the multiple ambiguities of the importance statement. Have we done this because we are embarrassed by our confessional past, or fearful that there is still a confessional ghost in our educational machine? Mindful that a statement of the rationale must eschew lists of content or skills, and instead lay a convincing claim for the subject to have a place at the educational table, we in RE could be more honest and bold about what we seek for pupils. Much of what we presently claim as the rationale – interpreting ideas, asking questions, respecting difference – stops short of any ultimate destination. It might be that we want the learners to be able to do these things in order to know more about God, to love and revere him more fully; or to have a generally spiritual and reflective outlook on life; or to be wise and discerning as between truth and falsehood. The first of these purposes could only work as a rationale in schools with a theistic religious ethos, and even in those contexts it is recognized as problematic;[20] the second and third would work in any school. It would be possible to argue that without such a purpose, without learning experiences explicitly oriented to this purpose, a person is not wholly educated. The examples offered – there are other candidates – are all bolder, more explicit and at the same time more focused than what we presently claim as our rationale.

Pedagogy and effectiveness

In paying attention to intended outcomes, a pedagogy of RE must also be specific and realistic about measurement of its effectiveness. This relates back to questions of the rationale, because the question of whether RE is effective raises the question 'for what?' The recent international research project titled 'Does RE work?' encountered this problem, with answers that were accordingly mixed.[21] On the aims, intentions and rationales of RE, the research team encountered 'a plethora of contested, frequently contradictory' answers.[22] Researchers speculated that the lack of consensus and shifting definitions of rationale might be revealing 'a preference for ambiguity over clarification', born of 'those collective anxieties that engulf a subject so regularly traduced as having no place in school education'.[23] However, it is just as likely to be the other way round, i.e. that being traduced and marginalized in the education system is in part the price RE pays for having a less than coherent educational rationale. This weakness is nowhere more fully exposed to the gaze of colleagues than in the normal definition of pupil progress.

It is a concern in all subjects that definitions of pupil progress must be coherently related to the subject's rationale and purpose. This relation is merely one link in a longer chain of pedagogical consequence which we discuss in Chapter 7. The questions 'Why are we teaching RE?' and 'What do we expect of our learners?' are intimately interrelated. They are questions that a school should ask, and to which it should have clear answers. Official curriculum documents, national and local, should also be clear on this. In England the model of expectation and progress has evolved to keep pace with the templates set by successive versions of the national curriculum. The majority of English RE uses a model derived from the work of a distinguished RE theorist and practitioner, Michael Grimmitt,[24] who identified the life-world of the learner and the life-world of the religion as being two major reference points that meet in RE, and argued that measures of effectiveness should derive from these two worlds. This led to the identification of two attainment targets for RE, learning about religion and learning from religion, which have been enshrined in the 2004 framework[25] and, to a lesser extent, in its 2008 successor,[26] with an eight-level scale of attainment for each target. The hegemony of this model is seen in its widespread use in nearly all local agreed syllabuses, exam specifications and textbooks. Much work has gone into promoting teacher understanding and use of the targets and the scale: this included applying the science of assessment for learning to the scale, and offering teachers specific assessment focuses.[27] In spite of the testimony of many teachers and consultants that the two attainment targets and the scale are a clear, workable and widely understood model of progression, there is evidence that this is not so.

The problem arises in having two targets (rather than one, as is common in most subjects other than English, mathematics and science). Two targets will inevitably divide and dilute effort, and set up – or perpetuate – tensions in the pedagogy of RE. The two targets are not understood in a unanimous way, some teachers believing them to be a demarcation of cognitive and affective processes, others associating them with distinct areas of content, while many teachers assume that the first target must precede the second. None of these assumptions appear in Grimmitt's original work, nor in the official documents, but they have grown up as ways of dealing with the duality of two targets. Further confusion is sown by the variances of expression: the official version, learning about/from religion, implies measurement of a study of the existence of religion as a personal and social reality that has impact on individuals and communities. But it has sometimes been rendered as learning about/from religions, meaning assessment of a study of separate belief systems, a fragmented and flawed approach. Occasionally the phrase has become learning about/from RE, indicating a notion that the measure of pupil progress in education is that they have learnt about and from their education, surely a tautologous and potentially narcissistic definition of progress. The result is a confusion so widespread that it calls into question the validity of the targets as a measure of effectiveness and progress.[28]

Other, deeper problems continue with the attainment targets. Inspectors expressed concern about the mismatch of content to targets seen in many locally agreed syllabuses. It has been quite common for syllabuses to adopt the eight-level scale, but without concomitantly changing the sequence or structure of content to be taught. This in practice made some syllabuses incoherent.[29] Viv Baumfield points up the design faults in having two targets that are separate and assumed to be sequential,[30] with the inevitable danger that, where assessment expectations point, teaching methods will follow: all too often, to teaching content first, and allowing discussion and reflection only second. Such a pattern suits the interests of religious groups, as it places the responses of learners into a position that is subordinate and contingent in relation to pre-determined religious content. Rare are the schemes that place the learners' views, questions and experiences first. More common are the lessons and units in which information retrieval is planned and assessed, then personal response is planned and assessed. Since they rarely engage with each other, the level of pupil attainment reported for 'about' might be divergent from that of 'from'. In such circumstances, teachers have struggled to give pupils a single grade or level that is coherent, valid and meaningful, or have over-rewarded work that is predominantly descriptive.[31] It is almost as if two subjects were being taught and assessed in the same period.

It is instructive to ask any RE practitioner what their reaction would be if they had to choose only one of the two attainment targets. Many teachers have a favourite, but nearly all would wish to compensate, for example by introducing into 'learning about' some opportunities to ask questions, experience, reflect, respond and consider how the students' learning has changed them. To avoid triviality or abstraction, any learning about must surely evoke depths of response in and of itself, without the need of a separate measurement; likewise, to save itself from ignorance or narcissism, any learning from must precede and follow investigation. This in practice suggests that many teachers could see the two targets as left and right steps in a single journey, guided by a single scale of measurement. In the QCDA 2010 proposals for a primary programme of study for RE,[32] a single cyclical set of learning skills was envisaged, essentially unifying the two targets. In one locally agreed syllabus,[33] a single attainment target, highly attuned to a rationale and pedagogy of interpreting religion in relation to human experience, has succeeded in changing practice. It has, therefore, been possible to envisage and operate alternatives to the two-target approach.

A duality that separates rigorous investigation from personal response sets up the possibility of dishonest and disappointing enquiries into religion and belief. The about/from duality increases the distance between information and reflection, thereby cheapening the conclusions of enquiry. Too often, Hollywood endings characterize RE planned in this way: it does not matter that we or the learners disagree, because we can all respect each other's point of view. Thus the most widely claimed virtue of RE, tolerance, collapses into intolerance of intolerance, and its boast of controversy becomes banality. The separation of 'learning from' requires that all enquiries end positively, all explanation of religion be respectful, all analysis concludes with underlying unity, all personal conclusions be irenic. Philip Barnes's critique of pedagogies and documents that promote a liberal strategy as being dishonest and ineffective – he argues that the liberal model succeeds only in its capacity to 'demonize' exclusive positions and those who hold them[34] – is far from true of all RE lessons, but the about/from separation makes it more possible.

Given these design faults, why does about/from still hold such a popular position with many practitioners? Could it be that the duality serves as a compromise between opposing rationales for the subject? English RE has a complicated evolutionary history, with many opposing models of the subject. Like a family whose ancient quarrels are not quite forgotten, RE seeks at any cost to maintain the peace. Having evolved from a cultural form of confessional and nurture-based pedagogy, through a misplaced application of phenomenological methods, RE has found peace in a balanced formula that intentionally enshrines both traditions. The claimed objectivity of informational study, and the preserved possibility of being influenced by that which one studies, are neatly brought together in a pairing of about and from. We have here a blend which mixes the understanding of religious traditions with the personal development of the learner. This attempts to resolve the conflict between phenomenological and confessional models, a conflict which is itself a proxy war for the longer struggle between religious and secular worldviews. The attempt at resolution is not for reasons of pedagogical coherence but to maintain the unity of the subject community. About/from also attempts to cover the tendentious claims made by both models – for phenomenological, that it could be objective,[35] and for confessional, that it could be effective.[36] The pairing of the two targets has papered over the cracks, rather than resolving these underlying arguments. The pressure of changing assessment practices and the scrutiny of inspectors has made the cracks more visible and leads to the conclusion that progress and standards in RE cannot be meaningfully and reliably measured by two parallel processes.

About/from, as a measure of effectiveness in pupil progress, carries the same hallmarks of compromise and ambiguity as the importance statement. Rationales and external standards should be consistent with each other, but preferably on the basis of shared clarity and realism. English RE's dominant existing statements have served well enough to introduce a limited amount of consensual agreement on purposes and levels of expectation, but the classroom practice built from them has been muddled, and the inherent design faults and the wider educational climate require us to move on from them. We now have the prospect of an end to the generic eight-level scales as being muddled, incoherent and burdensome,[37] and an opportunity to be set free from the duality of our two attainment targets, seeking instead a simpler, clearer but no less valid purpose and measure.

Conclusion

We see that religious education is pedagogically ambiguous, whether in the context of maintained community schools consciously catering for all learners or that of schools with a religious ethos. There are important political reasons for the ambiguity, which has allowed RE to be a big tent of cultural traditionalists, confessionalists, theologians, inter-religious anti-secularists, secularists, phenomenologists, social scientists, pedagogical progressives, personal development practitioners and no doubt some others, all working together to advocate RE. Ambiguity can be useful, and the semblance of unanimity has allowed RE to grow in certain ways. However, the inherent tensions in key official documents feed through to schizophrenic practice and poor definitions of progression. This lack of clarity is compounded by the reality that many teachers lack the time and inclination to ask the theoretical questions that could clarify their own pedagogy. Into this vacuum come the suspicions of our colleagues from other subjects, head teachers and some parents, that what we are about is educationally improper and covertly confessional. Thus, it is said, we are not a legitimate subject. RE in most schools is less improper than the suspicious critics imagine, but still less proper, and less clear, than it could be.

The next two chapters argue in greater depth how this pedagogical problem remains in several of the constructs of RE that are currently proposed. This starts with a critique of the dominant phenomenological model started by Ninian Smart and its extension into an ethnographic approach (Chapter 4). Then we shall consider the problems inherent in other approaches, such as the dialogic approach championed by Robert Jackson and the critical realist approach championed by Andrew Wright (Chapter 5).

Response from Clive Erricker

In this chapter Mark has carried out a much needed critique of the inability of the RE community to release itself from its confessional burden and rigorously identify its educational credentials. That this has been a long time in coming points to the shallowness of pedagogical engagement within the subject and the determination to ensure it represents religion rather than educational goals. In a way it is surprising that our educational colleagues have often been so supportive of us, but often on misguided grounds. So often I have heard history teachers remark on the value of religious studies (alongside their own subject discipline) but they don't say religious *education*. I often wonder whether they were providing us with a convenient academic camouflage because there are significant distinctions between the rationale pursued in the academy for religious studies and those pursued in the educational world for RE. Sometimes head teachers commend RE as an important subject on the curriculum (though the opposite is also the case), but I rarely hear them voice an effective rationale for the subject. It often seems they are taken in by claims for its inclusivity and attempts to address community cohesion and diversity without any deeper analysis of its integrity.

What Mark asks us to do is deal with the mixed inheritance of RE, clarify its rationale and make clear what we recognize as its educational purpose.

Chapter 4

Phenomenology and anthropology

The advocacy of religion as an approach to RE

Clive Erricker

Opening story

It was RE inspection day, and it started with a meeting between the inspector and six students across years 7–11. The inspector asked: 'Do you know why you are here?' Nobody knew, so he explained that this was an RE inspection and he wanted their views on the RE they were taught. This started the discussion; some students, the older ones, were very willing to give their views, some were silent or just said something if they were asked by name (mainly the younger ones). The inspector had trouble learning one of the names because it was unusual and the student only spoke very quietly; nevertheless the inspector felt that it didn't do much for the student's confidence that he asked him to repeat it and got it wrong first time.

The students were very positive about RE:

- 'It is really good. We learn about different religions and people's backgrounds and about the holocaust and why things happened.'
- 'We learn other people's different views.'
- 'RE supplements other subjects; we need to know about culture too.'
- 'We are asked for our opinions and we discuss community cohesion.'
- 'It has changed my understanding; for example I didn't know about the diversity in Christianity.'
- 'RE is important, but not the most important subject.'

When they left one student said to the inspector 'You are not going to sack our teacher are you?'

The students were positive about RE and it was obviously taught pretty well but the inspector was left with some reservations:

- Why were all the students positive not only about RE, but also about religion?
- Why did they comment favourably on being asked their opinions in RE, but say nothing about the skills it demanded of them, such as critical thinking (though one did say they were asked to 'reason')?
- Why was knowing about diversity a good thing but the issues that diversity raises not mentioned?
- Why was RE associated with culture rather than religion by one of the students?
- What was it that made some other subjects more important than RE?

The inspector was also uneasy about some of the other factors in this meeting. He was aware that the power relations between him and the students were obviously influential and was struck by the fact that one student thought he had the power to sack their teacher. He was concerned that some students were far more articulate than others. Shouldn't the need to be articulate be a basic ingredient of their education? How was that addressed, or wasn't it? Why couldn't they, when asked, say more about how they were assessed and how that was related to their learning? What, exactly, did they think the point of their learning in RE was?

All of these factors, of course, provided issues he pursued during the rest of his inspection when he observed lessons, scrutinized planning and assessments and interviewed teachers. But what struck him most forcibly was the way in which the students' responses were formed from an acceptance of the idea of multiculturalism and the premises upon which anthropological and phenomenological enquiry were pursued: acceptance of difference.

Introduction

This chapter analyses the predominant methods that have informed the teaching of religious education in community schools over the last 30 to 40 years: these are phenomenology, as conceived by Ninian Smart, and anthropology or ethnography. It argues that these descriptive approaches actually work in the same fashion and to the same end: the representation of religion as liberal and benign. As a result, they operate in the service of multicultural policy. The chapter concludes that this representation is at best partial and at worst misleading, with the result that religious education became little more than a vehicle for nurture into Western liberal values.

Phenomenology and Smart's desideratum

Perhaps the clearest exponent of the notion that religion should serve a non-ideological cause, and has the resources to do so, was Ninian Smart, who provided the basis of the phenomenological approach to religious education prevalent in England and Wales. He stated:

> A multicultural or pluralistic philosophy of religion is a desideratum, and it is amazing how culture-bound so many Western philosophers have been: an unconscious (to be kind) imperialism. ... We have surely passed beyond a stage in human life when national values stand supreme, after all the horrors national wars have caused during this passing century ... a kind of spiritual democracy should eliminate inter-religious and inter-ideological violence. ... We need an overarching worldview for all human beings.[1]

Smart's desideratum is instructive. Based upon an historical backdrop of the Cold War and then the euphoria of the fall of the Berlin Wall and the Soviet Union and Fukuyama's *End of History* (which Fukuyama has since rescinded) and proceeding from a twentieth century riven with nationalist conflict, it provided a new and different vision. But the twenty-first century teaches us otherwise. A democratic non-ideological worldview embraced by the agency of religion to overcome inter-ideological violence and to create a spiritual democracy no longer seems credible. Religions, as some of the main agents in the creation of ideological conflicts, seem the least likely candidates, and democracy itself has been compromised by its ideological free-market capitalist, neo-liberal, imperialist and exploitative tendencies.

However, what this should teach us is that competing ideologies are not just religious but also secular, and that the enemies of Smart's 'spiritual democracy' reside in all such ideologies, religious or not.

Smart, however, was voicing a hope rather than a reality, and that in turn became the basis of an approach to religious education.[2] Thus, the aim was not to investigate the phenomenon of religion as it was but according to what was understood as its potential. As a result, it was the method employed that resulted in the representation produced. For example, by employing epoche (restraint or suspension of judgement, also referred to as 'bracketing out') and eidetic vision (the ability to see what is really there or objectively present as a result of employing epoche), Smart also promoted the cultivation of empathy (being able to see the world from the believer's point of view). This approach does, of course, mitigate the danger of stereotyping and misinformation because it forces researchers/students to recognize that their own cultural lenses and value systems will distort perception unless put to one side.

However, there is a tension here. Smart also states that '[t]he study of religion must attempt to be objectively outlined in a warm way ... that serves the insider as well as the outsider.'[3] What Smart refers to as a 'warm way' enables the appreciation of the beliefs and behaviours of the subject of study to be observed and better represented without cultural distortion on the part of the researcher/student. This could be regarded as objectivity, but not in the sense of the natural sciences. However, the situatedness of the researcher/ student as a 'second' subject has to be acknowledged and the method employed in the approach predisposes the researcher/student toward a positive appreciation of the subject of study. In itself, this does not present itself as a problem within the research paradigm used. What it does call into question is the limitations of the use of the paradigm. This will become clearer below when we study the analogous anthropological/ethnographic method that has also been employed in the study of religion and has influenced religious education.

The representation of religions and (socio-)anthropological method

Claude Lévi-Strauss, the father of the structuralist approach to anthropological enquiry, provides us with a useful introduction to the politics of anthropology and whether that can be applied to the study of religion, and as a result to religious education:

> Behind the two divergent attitudes of the anthropologist who is a critic at home and a conformist abroad, there lies, then, another contradiction from which he finds it even more difficult to escape. If he wishes to contribute to the improvement of his own community, he must condemn social conditions similar to those he is fighting against, wherever they exist, in which case he relinquishes his objectivity and impartiality. Conversely, the detachment to which he is constrained by moral scrupulousness and scientific accuracy prevents him criticizing his own society, since he is refraining from criticizing any one society in order to acquire knowledge of them all. Action within one's own society precludes understanding of other societies, but a thirst for universal understanding involves renouncing all possibility of reform.[4]

Here Lévi-Strauss is pointing to the difficulty involved in adhering to anthropological method as a scrupulously scientific means for describing and presenting specific communities other than one's own while also being a critic of certain societal practices within one's own society and that of others, which demand reform on the basis of ethical principles (for example, such as those of human rights). The anthropologist can report but cannot judge. All forms of society that the anthropologist studies have to be given equal validity. However, this approach, one of 'cultural relativism' often associated with Franz Boas, is predicated on a critique of certain of Western society's values, most significantly ethnocentricity.

However, if we compare what Lévi-Strauss says, at the time of writing, with the responses of the students in our opening story above, we can note that they have learned to be the opposite of what the anthropologist understands as his conundrum, but over 50 years later. Ironically, they have learned to be conformists at home (conformists to the values based in what they are taught) without any, or very little in some cases, experience of being 'abroad'. They regard diversity as a positive (religio-) cultural phenomenon to be affirmed. How did this happen? This shift in socio-cultural values is, in part, explained by the comments in the article that follows which identifies the use of a descriptive or 'cultural relativist' approach in anthropology (perhaps better described as ethnography) which has come to dominate our teaching in liberal education.

As Lila Abu-Lughod writes in 'Do Muslim women really need saving?' on the subject of the burqa:

> Ultimately, the significant political-ethical problem the burqa raises is how to deal with cultural 'others.' How are we to deal with difference without accepting the passivity implied by the cultural relativism for which anthropologists are justly famous – a relativism that says it's their culture and it's not my business to judge or interfere, only to try to understand. Cultural relativism is certainly an improvement on ethnocentrism and the racism, cultural imperialism, and imperiousness that underlie it; the problem is that it is too late not to interfere. The forms of lives we find around the world are already products of long histories of interactions.[5]

However, interference and making judgements can be seen as a continuation of that very cultural imperialism that cultural relativism opposes. This anthropological problem is also a larger political one for Western states, that extends into their forms of education. What principles should be applied to the representation of particular groups in one's own society and those of others? Abu-Lughod's article proceeds to show how the wearing of the burqa represents one of these 'long histories of interactions' in commenting on the Taliban and Afghanistan:

> First, it should be recalled that the Taliban did not invent the burqa. It was the local form of covering that Pashtun women in one region wore when they went out. The Pashtun are one of several ethnic groups in Afghanistan and the burqa was one of many forms of covering in the subcontinent and Southwest Asia that has developed as a convention for symbolizing certain women's modesty or respectability. The burqa, like some other forms of 'cover' has, in many settings, marked the symbolic separation of men's and women's spheres, as part of the general association of women with family and home, not with public space where strangers mingled.
>
> Twenty years ago the anthropologist Hanna Papanek, who worked in Pakistan, described the burqa as 'portable seclusion'.[6] She noted that many saw it as a liberating invention because it enabled women to move

out of segregated living spaces while still observing the basic moral requirements of separating and protecting women from unrelated men. Ever since I came across her phrase portable seclusion, I have thought of these enveloping robes as 'mobile homes.' Everywhere, such veiling signifies belonging to a particular community and participating in a moral way of life in which families are paramount in the organization of communities and the home is associated with the sanctity of women.

What had happened in Afghanistan under the Taliban is that one regional style of covering or veiling, associated with a certain respectable but not elite class, was imposed on everyone as 'religiously' appropriate, even though previously there had been many different styles, popular or traditional with different groups and classes – different ways to mark women's propriety, or, in more recent times, religious piety.[7]

But this uncritical commentary on histories of interactions excludes any sense of the political and sites of power. What if she said 'mobile prisons' instead of 'mobile homes'?[8] How come there is no critical comment on the Taliban making all women wear the burqa? What if we were to write all social histories in this way? At what point do you stop describing and start opposing, e.g. where there is a lack of agency and voice allowed for a certain group, whether ethnic or gender?[9] We must bear in mind that agency and voice are formed within an overarching, shifting socio-political context involving power. The question is: who has the power and therefore makes the rules, even if they give a marginal advance in freedom to certain groups? Additionally, therefore, for example, if my modesty and honour are preserved in this context why would I not speak for it rather than against it, despite the fact that in other ways it might still be a way in which my rights are curtailed?

Abu-Lughod goes on to remark on the situation of Afghan women refugees:

The *New York Times* carried an article about Afghan women refugees in Pakistan that attempted to educate readers about this local variety [of different forms of covering].[10] The article describes and pictures everything from the now iconic burqa with the embroidered eyeholes, which a Pashtun woman explains is the proper dress for her community, to large scarves they call chadors, to the new Islamic modest dress that wearers refer to as hijab. Those in the new Islamic dress are characteristically students heading for professional careers, especially in medicine, just like their counterparts from Egypt to Malaysia. One wearing the large scarf was a school principal; the other was a poor street vendor. The telling quote from the young street vendor is, 'If I did [wear the burqa] the refugees would tease me because the burqa is for "good women" who stay inside the home.'[11] Here you can see the local status associated with the burqa – it is for good respectable women from strong families who are not forced to make a living selling on the street.[12]

We can add to this further information and comment. The reason why the burqa was introduced as a legal requirement and common dress for women was because many of the Taliban men were Pashtun and they universalized their own custom because it was considered necessary for modesty; i.e. it was a particularly rigid code imposed upon other women also.

The further point is that it was traditional for only 'middle-class' women to wear the burqa, an elevation in terms of modesty and status conferred. It isn't that Islam in the Qur'an demands the burqa, since it is not mentioned. It is that certain forms of Islam have imposed hard-line interpretations of modesty and honour that accord with the importance of those concepts within the Qur'an and early Islam.

Here we might ask, is there no critical commentary to be made on these restrictions of agency and class distinctions in relation to status based on the symbolization of dress? At what point do you start asking why there is no equivalent of Friere's project of conscientization? And, if this were to emerge, should it be as a result of initiatives taking place in Afghan society, or be initiated by Western educators?

There are also further questions to be asked, premised on the fact that the burqa and similar forms of covering have become a test of loyalty or authenticity for a minority of Muslims in some Western societies. What questions does that raise about minority cultures and their capacity to critique and renew themselves, on the one hand, and majority Western cultures and their capacity or need to adapt to this phenomenon? Clearly, given the diverse responses of the latter, there are still very difficult questions to engage with that the mantras of multiculturalism, such as acceptance of diversity, are not sufficiently equipped to deal with, given the complexities of this situation. The reason is that the values systems that underpin the differences involved do not lie just at the level of tolerance but work down into the principles that underpin societies and their sense of integrity.

What Abu-Lughod has done is to provide an informative socio-historical record of why Muslim women have forms of covering, especially the burqa. Implicit in this is a refusal to make any critical comment on these forms of historical interactions that she presents. And that is appropriate in relation to the values of the discipline in which she is employed. In effect her explanation is a form of cultural apologetics – identifying difference without feeling the need to make an evaluative assessment of it. This form of apologetics feels itself justified on the basis of the ignorance it confronts (an example of Lévi-Strauss' conformist abroad and critic at home). That is well and good, in so far as it enlightens and informs, but that cannot itself be a basis for its full justification.

It would certainly be a plus for our students in schools to be able to present this information in opposition to racist comments and mono-culturally misinformed opinions but it does not solve the larger question of whether requiring women to wear the burqa is justified in our context, or in any context, or whether it is appropriate for some cultures to regard women's role as being restricted in public life. Whilst, later, Abu-Lughod generally speaks of the need for the anthropologist to work with groups that may be seeking change in order that those groups may be able to best organize to represent themselves, she opposes the idea that Westerners should think they can best represent those groups' interests by, for example, declaring that burqa-wearing women should be identified as enslaved or in need of freedom/saving. However, the idea of working with groups seeking change takes the anthropologist beyond the original remit of reporting descriptively on specific cultures and their underlying social structures. Her approach has been carried over into that adopted within the socio-anthropological approach to religious education.

Dialogue and democratic values

We can find similar approaches to the idea that support for change should be through dialogue with and support for particular religious groups in, for example, Wilna A.J. Meier's *Tradition and Future of Islamic Education*[13] and Saba Mahmood's *Politics of Piety: The Islamic revival and the feminist subject*.[14] The accent is on reform within the tradition itself developed from its own hermeneutical possibilities. For example, in Meier's study, she researches other traditions of learning in Islam than those present within dominant forms of Islam today. In doing so the concept of *ijtihad* becomes central for her. She states:

> Precisely this concept of *ijtihad* plays a salient role once more in the current context. When the relationship between Islam and modern Western culture is discussed by Muslims and Muslim intellectuals, this concept of independent individual judgement plays a determining role. Muslim modernists, devoted to the modernization and reform of Islam in and for the modern context ascribe a crucial role to *ijtihad*.[15]

For example:

> Irshad Manji ... is a striking advocate of Islamic reform ... she explains 'I am a Muslim Refusenik. That does not mean I refuse to be a Muslim; it simply means I refuse to join an army of automatons in the name of Allah. ... Her website is the voice of the Project Ijtihad, her foundation, located in New York, which wished to bring about 'a renaissance of critical thinking in Islam'.[16]

Meier continues, 'She is convinced, and I share this conviction, that this is the only path to an Islam that is viable and not a fossil.'[17]

This is certainly a step beyond cultural relativism but, at the same time, we can recognize that this is an attempt at dialogue through aligning similar liberal ideas found in Western liberal democracies and in Islamic tradition.

We might say it is a dialogue based on forms of liberalism that the Western anthropologist, scholar or educator seeks to encourage toward the formation of 'democratic Islam'. At the same time Western Islamophobia is discredited because it only takes account of militant, fundamentalist Islam. But what is going on here is an attempt to discredit forms of religious fundamentalism and highlight possibilities of reform based on a more liberal and democratic spirit within religious traditions. In other words, reformed Islam/religion needs to look and think more like the liberal culture of the West.

Educationally, we could well learn from this but it does not present a recognizable representation of the majority expressions of Islam that we should, in all honesty, offer to our students. What it does suggest is that Islam is not wholly adverse to the values of liberal democracy and that that tendency can be fostered. In other words, we can still see the influence of Smart's desideratum.

When teachers teach religion they are too often in the business of presenting forms of religion that appeal to the Western liberal sentiment that they seek to nurture in their students. We can see evidence of this in the students' remarks about RE in the story at the beginning of this chapter. What they often fear and are trying to disguise is that religion can be nasty as well as nice. Also, just as the burqa article tries to do, they want to represent religious difference in a benign, descriptive way that encourages tolerance.

It could be argued that, at heart, we have a deeply biased attitude, paternalistic and colonial, that paradoxically presumes the superiority of the society that the anthropologist/researcher represents over and above the society studied; that is why the latter needs defending. We might also say that the assumption of not criticizing is underpinned by the assumption of superiority and an absence of dialogue with those who are not disposed to our values and notions such as equality.

Why the study of religion is not the same as ethnography

Ethnography and anthropology as the study of different peoples and cultures is quite different from the study of religions as institutionalized systems, which is not to say that religions do not have an effect on peoples and cultures. They obviously interact, as was clear in Abu-Lughod's study above. However, religious systems have their own hermeneutical frameworks that are designed to reinforce themselves, even if they transmute when interacting with different cultures. Buddhism demonstrates a certain elasticity in this respect in its journey to China, Japan and the West, for example. But some systems are more elastic than others.

Returning to Lévi-Strauss, he distinguishes in his comments between the anthropological approach employed in the research into different cultures and the approach he employs when commenting specifically on different religions. For example, his contrasting comments on Islam and Buddhism are significant:

The whole of Islam would, in fact, seem to be a method for creating insurmountable conflicts in the minds of believers, with the proviso that a way out can subsequently be found by adopting extremely simple (but over-simple) solutions. With one hand they are rushed to the brink of danger; with the other they are held back at the edge of the abyss. If a man is worried about the virtue of his wives and daughters while he is away campaigning, what simpler solution could he find than to veil them and lock them away? This explains the development of the modern burkah which ... looks like some orthopaedic apparatus.[18]

Also:

If one were looking for a barrack room religion, Islam would seem to be the ideal solution; strict observance of rules ... detailed inspections and meticulous cleanliness ... masculine promiscuity both in spiritual matters and in the carrying out of the organic functions; and no women.[19]

Of Buddhism, or more specifically the Buddha, he writes:

What else, indeed, have I learned from the masters who taught me, the philosophers I have read, the societies I have visited and even from that science which is the pride of the West, apart from a few scraps of wisdom which, when laid end to end, coincide with the meditation of the Sage at the foot of the tree?[20]

We might say that the contrasting judgements that he makes are based upon the values of Western liberalism. He views the rule-bound, totalitarian structure of Islamic obedience negatively when compared with the enquiring nature of the Buddha's search for an end to suffering. This points to the need to recognize that it is not helpful to simply speak of religion as an over-arching category that can be addressed educationally as either good or bad. It is more nuanced than that. Also, unlike ethnographic studies of different localized cultures, the study of religions is a study of pervasive systems of thought immersed in and influential within a global context.

It can be claimed that *Tristes Tropiques*, from which Lévi-Strauss' comments are taken, is not, as such, an anthropological work but a memoir. Even so, the point Lévi-Strauss makes about the anthropologist's dilemma earlier is significant. It relates to the relationship between a professional role in one's discipline and one's fuller commentary on human affairs. In that respect his comments on Islam and the Buddha reveal his judgements on the extent to which differing teachings in religions contribute to the fulfilment of being human and the nature of the societies we create in relation to that. In a separate passage he meditates on the failure of the caste system in India to fulfil the original design of creating equal but different spaces in society for different groups.[21] However, the overarching question he leaves the educator with is how to present information and how to encourage students to make informed judgements that go beyond (but nevertheless include) the findings and methods of the discipline of anthropology. In religious education, religions have been treated such that this need is not appropriately addressed. This is an impoverishment in educational aim – students (and citizens) are not just anthropologists any more than they are just historians or geographers.

Additionally, what this analysis teaches us is that there is no objective place to stand. Once that is admitted then one's own values have to be affirmed at the outset of any enquiry, but these are not to be suspended as in the idea of bracketing out or empathizing or as a means to recognizing one's own subjectivity. Yes, the latter has to be reflexively observed but eventually one must then place the subject of study that has been enquired into and represented alongside/in relation to one's own values. And this becomes the next, critical or critiquing stage of the enquiry – How am I positioned in relation to the values of the subject of study and why? How do I defend differences and contrasts that have emerged? What actions are now possible/necessary as a result? This is what enquiry in a democratic classroom should look like.

Socio-anthropology versus the study of religious systems

The value of the project of anthropology has been to show that a-priori 'indigenous' or 'ethnic' societies (defined in the broad sense of different peoples or cultures rather than by skin colour) are not inferior to modern Western ones. But this has then been transferred to the investigation of modern religious groups, as though the two were synonymous in their organizational structure, values and provenance. As a result the metanarrative derived from the socio-anthropological approach is that both 'indigenous' or 'ethnic' cultures and religious systems are inherently positive. This has resulted in the judgement that the latter offer diversity to otherwise mono-cultural societies in the West (but through expressing ethnic culture). This is a bit confusing. The suggested parallel between the two is not sufficiently examined. Religious minority cultures in Western societies may or may not offer new and positive capital in democratic environments. What is lacking is an evaluation of that contribution. However, a multicultural policy, especially in the UK, renders this evaluation impossible, despite the fact that we know that certain forms of religion have been ideologically instrumental in undermining Western democracies and have been resisting democracy globally. The fundamental error resides in transferring anthropological enquiry into 'indigenous' or 'ethnic' societies and minority and vulnerable groups to the analysis of religion in the modern world. Academically speaking, we require a different evaluative method of enquiry. In relation to local, national and global intelligence we must evaluate the positive and negative impact of religious forms in relation to the possibilities of the democratic project.[22] The opposition to this tends to reside in a liberal position that suggests that different modi vivendi (ways of life) or political systems may be commensurable despite having diverse expressions. This position opposes forms of liberal 'imperialism' or 'ideological liberalism' that seek to impose Western 'universal' values upon others.

However, there is a political naiveté at work here, There is a tendency not to comment on religious ideologies. Ultimately, there is a necessity to impose certain human rights that democratic societies uphold on religiously framed systems that oppose them. To fail to do so would set back the progress achieved within Western democracies over the last 200 years, since the emergence of the European Enlightenment. In other words the positive changes that have come about in that time have to be extended into a global environment. Nevertheless, we have to be quite sure about what we mean by positive. I am not asserting that changes produced within Western democratic societies and imported into other societies have been uniformly positive; that would certainly not be the case.

The socio-anthropological approach to religion seeks to focus on 'religion on the ground' rather than religious ideologies because it understands the ideologists to be the imperialists who have prevented the recognition of groups that do not reflect their projection of religion or have denied the value of their indigenous culture. A typical case is that of Hinduism presented through the lens of Brahmanism and Vedanta. This does not accord with the many regional and tribal practices in India that are often derived from Dravidian rather than Vedic origins. As a result it has been claimed that even the construct of Hinduism is false and largely maintained as a nineteenth-century Orientalist fiction based on the notion of religion as 'isms' rather than the idea that belief permeates cultures in differing ways. There is value in this approach but it cannot disguise the fact that the 'isms' do exist and that they are highly influential. If, therefore, on the grounds of socio-anthropological enquiry you wish to present the religio-cultural forms as the basis of the representation of religion you run the inevitable risk of avoiding the powerful ideological religious presences that are a shaping force.[23]

Even worse, since in religious education you cannot avoid the importance of some of these ideological forms, as is the case with Vatican Roman Catholicism, it then gets dressed up in a socio-anthropological way: studying the practices of believers 'on the ground' and in their everyday life as though there were no political and ideological context in which these occur. You also get textbooks published, such as those in the *Faith in Action* series on Pope John Paul II and Mother Teresa which are hagiographic in character and, by default, therefore represent a form of religious nurture and an uncritical promotion of the value of these individuals.[24] What we might term a sub-socio-anthropological approach has been in widespread use as a deceptive strategy, giving the credentials of objectivity to studies that are too sympathetic to the beliefs, organizations or practices studied.

Our attempts to deny the presence and influence of religious ideologies have been counterproductive to an understanding of religion. Popular academic works such as the publications of Karen Armstrong have done much to affirm the idea that real religion is not doctrinal religion but forms of pietistic faith. She represents this in her distinction between mythos and logos and her affirmation of the apophatic tradition, which goes beyond language into silence.[25] This is a polemical position within the internal struggles of religion to define its 'true' nature. It is also a liberal position that wishes to deny the primacy of doctrinal and ideological religious forms. It serves to reinforce the socio-anthropological approach commented upon above. It is an interesting point for debate but it certainly should not define our understanding of religion. Mythos can serve ideological ends as well as logos, as Shlomo Sand comments:

> Each of us has assimilated multiple narratives shaped by past ideological struggles. ... various spheres of memory coalesce into an imagined universe representing the past, and it coalesces well before a person has acquired the tools for thinking critically about it.[26]

He goes on to argue in his thesis that the idea of Jewish expulsion from their homeland by the Romans created a myth of a right to return, whereby the state of Israel was established. And yet, he claims, the events of history do not bear out this expulsion nor, due to proselytization in 'exile', the 'prestige of belonging by birth to the chosen people'.[27] But:

> it was no accident that modern Jewish nationalism, opted for the fictitious element of the long tradition ... a linear timeline, along which, back and forth, from past to present and back again, moved a unique nation – wandering isolated, and, of course, quite imaginary.[28]

In other words this is a triumph of myth over history for ideological purposes.

Religions as systems

John Bowker has been the principal protagonist of the systemic nature of religions: they abide by systems created over long periods of time, which they have to preserve. He has also pointed out that this leads to them becoming dangerous once threatened on their borders.[29] These borders can be pressured geographically by political/economic change or through being asked to integrate into other societies because of migration. These religious systems are conceptually constructed and provide integrated conceptual ideologies. He maintains that such systems are naturally conservative and also, when threatened, seek to preserve their fundamentals, i.e. they become more fundamentalist. This can help to explain why concepts such as modesty and honour which underpin the wearing of the burqa or veiling and provide specific capital for women within the societies in which veiling is a particular expression of those concepts have become subject to a more particular and literalist expression of those concepts under the Taliban and other regimes. Veiling or cover in this extreme form is not a requisite to preserve modesty and honour in other socio-cultural contexts. It is the particular combination of forms of Islam and socio-political contexts that produces that interpretation, and such contexts can contain other pervasive conceptual influences – for example patriarchy.[30]

Similarly, Regis Debray writes that religions become intolerant when there is a:

> throbbing sense of insecurity. ... Every collective belief will tend towards fanaticism as soon as it sees itself threatened with disappearance, minority status or siege. Intolerance ... is the weak man's weapon against the strong. ... And polite indifference towards those other than oneself is the surest indication of a position of hegemony. It is easy to respect those from whom one has nothing to fear. ... For tolerance, the supreme good, is first of all a luxury, dependent on power relations. ... The Islam of Granada could turn a smiling face to all. That of Kabul is hateful.[31]

Conclusion: is religious education an apologetic for Western liberal values?

In relation to religious education in England and Wales and, it can be said, in other countries with Western value systems in education such as Hong Kong, Australia and New Zealand, there is a conspicuous attempt to defend religion and, in this respect, also in Europe, religious educators tend to act as apologists for religion. Smart, in part, provides the rationale for this and socio-anthropological/ethnographic approaches confirm this legacy. But you cannot do this without making judgement calls on the way in which religions manifest their presence in the world.

In Chapter 1, I spoke of 'offshore' ideologies. 'Offshore' in relation to religious groups means those groups that will not conform to the democratic laws and conventions of secular or pluralist nation states or international bodies, or which do so only selectively and conditionally. Their special pleading is based on their claim to a different and higher authority and a political and social system that proceeds from that authority. Therefore 'offshore' needs to be contextualized. In this case it refers to those groups who wish to ensure democratic regulation does not affect them. Some readers might have some sympathy with this. Consider the hegemony of modern secular democratic states in the West and their desire to impose this hegemony globally. This has often involved coercive if not corrupt strategies, in situations where resistance has been met, and dubious legality as well (consider the case of the war on Iraq). In so doing it has also involved the imposition of dictators (for example in Latin America), the support for corrupt, undemocratic regimes (for example in North Africa and the Middle East on the basis of the pursuit of wealth and desire for influence). In effect this amounts to imperial activity. Therefore a safe haven, to protect from all that, would seem desirable. This is what self-regulation and establishing one's own jurisdiction provides. On the other hand forms of religion are also involved in this ideological realpolitik. Religious fundamentalism, returning to the fundamentals when under threat, is an understandable response and often a valuable rallying call to citizens who otherwise would be indifferent, or even opposed, to such a characterization of their faith.

There is no subject that is more politically engaged in the contemporary world than that of religion. Despite this, religious education studiously seeks to avoid an acknowledgement of this state of affairs. It is as if religions are above political events. In seeking to offer this representation of religions, an idealized and decontextualized representation is constructed that presents religions in the mirror image of Western democratic values (again idealized and decontextualized) through the lionization of specific iconic 'religious' but 'democratic' figures such as Anne Frank, Martin Luther King, Mother Teresa, Gandhi and Aung San Suu Kyi as representatives of innocence, freedom, democracy, sanctity and non-violence. This is not an argument against the virtue of those individuals: it is a questioning of why they have been selected for study when other facets of the religious communities to which they belong, facets less consistent with Western values, have not. This selection also suggests a perverse desire to sanctify the standing of Western secularized societies through their support for 'religious' values. All this despite the fact that the founders of major world religions were immersed in the political affairs of their age – Jesus, Muhammad, the Buddha – as well as offering salvific messages. To say that they were not highly ideologically motivated, and their successors also, simply does not do justice to the nature of religion. Whilst a distinction is often registered between religion and politics, and another between the true face of religion and its perverted manifestations, and a third distinction between religion and culture, these distinctions all seek to affirm the sort of religion we wish to present without due justification.

Any enquiry into religion has to test these distinctions, whether they are justified, and, if so, on what basis. Furthermore, there is no basis for test unless we reveal the criteria we would use. When it comes to the interrogation of sacred texts it is a matter of interpretation; when it comes to evaluating action in the world the same is true. Students need to be aware of this and be transparent as to why they make the judgements they then do. This is a long way from the religious education presently in place which could be described as a new confessional (Western democratic) nurture that has replaced the nurture in Christianity that could no longer be explicitly sustained in state schooling (although there is still some tendency in some schools to do this).

When we teach different denominations of Christianity we ask students to refrain from truth judgements, and similarly with branches of other religions. Yet we circumscribe the boundaries of what can be called authentic religion without any recognizable academic criteria. This raises the question: in what sense is religious education anything other than indoctrination into (self-proclaimed) Western democratic values? We might also add: to what extent does it represent more than a gloss on hypocrisy and power?

In Chapter 5, I critique further forms of RE that have become influential based on developments emerging from the models analysed in this chapter, or which are in opposition to it.

Response from Mark Chater

The argument presented above may be summarized thus: that the anthropological derivations of RE are compromised, and that the subject, consciously or not, has become what it always denied: a strategy of advocacy. That which is advocated in classrooms now is not Christianity alone, but a generally modernist religious or ethical outlook on life, subtly shaped to fall wholly within the parameters of Western, democratic, human-rights and rational assumptions. Any religious or ideological item failing to fit that shape is taken out and placed aside.

This might be true – and it might not matter that it is so. If we accept Lévi-Strauss's warning that there is no objective place to stand, we must then choose, as teachers, between several stances none of which is perfect. Amongst many possible stances, one might be the frank acknowledgement of a Western liberal agenda, even a Christian or other religious one. Perhaps it matters less what the stance is and more how open the teacher is prepared to be. Can a teacher give explicit notification – to self, colleagues, head teacher, parents and above all pupils – that the RE project in his/her hands is purposed to shape the profile of religion in positive ways? Is part of this openness a real acknowledgement that religion as a force, and each specific religion, has been edited so that its most democratic-friendly and tolerant facets are visible? Is the teacher prepared to face and discuss the weaknesses of this chosen stance, including with pupils, in ways that do not abuse his/her power? If so, perhaps that teacher has no less professional integrity, and can find a home in the Western model of RE.

Greater dangers are presented by teachers with unknown or undeclared stances, whose pedagogical implications have not been examined and required to account for themselves. This is essentially a problem of pedagogical understanding, which is developed in Chapter 7.

Chapter 5

Discourse and dissonance in contemporary paradigms of RE

Clive Erricker

Opening story

The teacher had set up a really fun lesson. The students had to divide into groups of detectives and solve the problem of whether the resurrection really happened. They were given three alternative possibilities:

- The Romans had removed the body from the tomb.
- The disciples had removed the body from the tomb.
- Jesus really was resurrected.

The students could infer other possibilities if they thought them likely. They were given a relevant text to examine from a gospel. Then they got on with it. At the end of the lesson a spokesperson from each group reported back on their conclusions having been fully engaged the whole time. Each group concluded that Jesus must have been resurrected and gave some reasons why – problem solved.

But the inspector watching still had some problems. If you were a detective trying to work out whether a stolen body was involved, you would have to work from empirical evidence. How could you come up with a supernatural solution? Do you go back to the police station and say 'No problem Sarge, it was resurrection all right.' As if that were the end of it.

Why did the students take on this task so eagerly and come up with such a comfortable conclusion that matched with a religious claim in a lesson on RE? Would they have done that in another subject? Why could they not see that detectives do not behave in that way and come to those sorts of conclusions? There was a fundamental lack of understanding as to how evidence is used and conclusions arrived at in the constabulary.

How did this lesson add to their theological knowledge or their recognition of different forms of truth claims? It seemed wholly confused in design. Even though fully engaged and wholly participatory the learning involved was just wrong. First, whilst this was presented as an open-ended investigation the students seemed to sense there was a right answer. Second, what was the rationale for this? For students to enjoy it or was there any deeper pedagogical strategy beneath the surface? Did the teacher expect this lesson to result in a defence of a religious truth claim and was that part of its point? Why is there a confusion between religious belief and empirical investigation in the way the lesson proceeded, and why didn't the teacher or any of the students realize that? Was it a way to show that religion is compatible with modern claims to knowledge and therefore that religious belief is wholly credible? Where was the theological scrutiny of the religious text: its provenance, its intention, its context?

This is all about discourse and dissonance in the practice of RE – what makes the subject credible and where does that credibility lie? Or is the subject just a way of defending the claims of religion?

Introduction

In the last chapter I argued that phenomenological and ethnographic/anthropological approaches to religious education are inadequate. First, on the grounds that they fail to allow for a full range of evaluative judgements to be made about religious forms; second, because they promote representations of religions that mirror the liberalism of those approaches. In this chapter we shall investigate how this situation can be improved and what obstacles lie in the way of that by referring to other contemporary authors on religion and theorists and researchers in RE and approaches they have developed.

What should be taught and how should students learn?

It is often argued that religious education is a unique or at least distinctive subject on the curriculum. Certainly it is different from other subjects but so are all subjects, so uniqueness or distinctiveness cannot reside in a categorical distinction that does not also pertain to other subjects. Yet often this is what is meant by those who seek to defend the importance of RE. RE is also often referred to as the Cinderella subject on the curriculum, by those trumpeting its importance. This appears to mean that its value is overlooked. Presumably, as with Cinderella herself, there is an expectation that RE will, in time, be recognized.

People who advance these arguments do not do so principally because RE is seen as having a particular academic integrity, as historians often assert for history; nor because it inculcates certain specific, intrinsic skills that are not available to the same degree in other subjects. Rather they tend to employ this opinion on the basis of the subject matter: without religious education students will not learn about religions; plus, it teaches or develops, as a result, the extrinsic 'skill' (more a capacity) for empathy. Latterly, this has also been extended to the promotion of community cohesion and celebration of pluralism (an extension and development of multiculturalism). The problem with all these defences of the curriculum credentials for RE is that they do not, in any way, identify the intrinsic skills or capacities that the subject promotes nor do they highlight the intrinsic academic value that the discipline brings to the overall project of education. The vacuum that resides can be summed up in this argument: if students learn about religions they will become more empathetic to others with different belief and cultural systems and recognize the importance of and enrichment that follows from living in a diverse society and this will result in them developing further the capacity for empathy and recognizing the need for community cohesion.

Why is this argument simply wrong? We can put it in this way. First, teachers start with what has to be taught. Second, there are no intrinsic skills to be developed. Third, there is no evaluative judgement to be made on the material presented. Fourth, there is no educational rationale to be followed in the development of students' progress. Fifth, there is no sense of religious education as an academic discipline. Sixth, as a result, teachers are confused as to what the second attainment target, 'learning from religion', could actually mean. Most teachers, therefore, interpret it as meaning becoming more empathetic toward the subject of study, religions, and exhibiting something equivalent to the values teachers present as within religions and correlating those with the values within students' own lives. Pedagogically this is totally insufficient and confused. Why is this so?

Note the way in which the approaches of phenomenology and ethnography/anthropology have imposed the importance of not making judgements on the subject of study. This is understandable in so far as it worked to mitigate misinformed mono-cultural bias against the strangeness of other belief systems, but it does not advance students' learning to the point where informed judgements on difference can be made. The presumption entailed is that any judgements are likely to be misinformed. This bias resides in the presumptions of the approaches entailed: they have no hermeneutical perspective that could be incorporated into educational practice that allows for judgements on difference or diversity. Essentially, the approaches employed have no capacity for critical reflection on the subjects of study. As a result many teachers of RE understand their role to be to induct or coerce students into the theoretical positions and assumptions that these approaches entail and are fearful of any critical responses, which they, either overtly or covertly, suppress. This, in turn, means that they suppress any critical thinking. At its worst it means they distinguish between right and wrong answers. Students quickly recognize the codes by which the discourse of the classroom proceeds. Below I analyse ways in which three other influential approaches to RE fail to do the subject justice: dialogic RE, RE as textual interpretation and RE based on truth claims.

Dialogic RE

It may be claimed that my description above can apply to misinformed and weak practice but not where the practice is informed by good research and theory. For example, the dialogic approach championed by Robert Jackson explicitly states that:

> pupils should be given the opportunity to study and reflect upon different religious and philosophical viewpoints in a structured way and to apply skills of interpretation and criticism methodologically.[1]

He adds, that dialogic approaches 'affirm the individual's democratic right to freedom of religion or belief and they actively promote tolerance of religious and ideological difference within the law'.[2]

Certainly, the approach has merit if, as Jackson points out, it aims to 'develop an understanding of the grammar ... of religions and the interpretive skills necessary to gain that understanding'.[3] Certainly it has merit if, as Jackson claims, it develops critical thinking. But, it cannot be claimed that via these aims the project is fulfilled because the overarching aim is being positive about and engaging with diversity. Therefore to the extent that the project is successful this last aim has to be fulfilled. It is such a broad aim (do I have to be positive about and engage with all forms of diversity?) and one that at the outset stipulates a disposition that will be instrumental to the criteria for success (therefore I may demonstrate the development of skills and critical thinking but that will not be enough).

The issue here is also one of what cannot be covered, ideologically/ religiously, because it will not submit to this procedure. This approach accommodates modernized religion rather than pre-modern religion. Note that there is no place for hostility to pre-modern religious manifestations of hostility to secularization except 'within the law', so no mention of offshore religion – which is effectively beyond the pale and the curriculum constraint. What is circumscribed in terms of the subject of study is religion that is willing to hold itself accountable to democracy – itself an ideology. As Jackson quotes appreciatively, from the *Parekh Report*, 'Procedural values are those that maintain the preconditions for democratic dialogue.'[4]

Thus, a religious form that follows the procedural values for democratic dialogue can participate – it can be a subject of study. But a form of religion that does not has no place. Representation of religions is subject to its dialogic value. This suggests that controversial forms of religion are not likely to be discussed and, as a result, those that can be discussed, are necessarily 'democratic' in form. Or, if the former are discussed, there will be a prior caveat on their value. It therefore also follows that the dialogic process in the classroom between teacher and students is meant to model that which can take place between religious representatives, using this process. This is meant to enable inclusivity but, of course, it also sets the markers for exclusion.[5] This exclusion can occur against forms of religion that do not recognize participation in the democratic discourse demanded, against students of the same view or against approaches to RE that do not subscribe to this approach. It is necessary to realize that this is not an epistemology-free model, despite the fact that Jackson lauds Cush's remarks on 'epistemological humility' and 'methodological agnosticism' and Cooling's comment that RE should 'encourage debate between people of very different and fundamentally opposed views and ... assist in the development of strategies which enable people to work together for the common good'.[6]

We need to be clear then that this approach to religious education is not about the representation of religion, per se. It is about encouraging participation toward the 'common good' in pluralist environments and societies. The conception of the 'common good' of course only makes sense in the context of 'diversity' trumping 'difference', or to put it another way, common values being understood as more important than epistemological differences. Ipgrave's work illustrates this in more detail with a three-step approach: primary dialogue – acceptance of diversity, difference and change; secondary dialogue – a positive approach to primary dialogue, characterized by an openness to difference; tertiary dialogue – the activity of dialogue itself, which draws upon primary and secondary dialogue (presumably the dispositions involved).[7] As a result, what we have is an approach that nurtures particular attitudes and accompanying skills of importance to democratic societies seeking to ensure that ideological difference does not affect community cohesion. We have to ask, therefore, what is the place in this project for religions that maintain pre-modern characteristics or approaches to knowledge, and for approaches to knowledge, such as post-modernism, that are sceptical of modernist designs?

In classrooms what we are likely to see (echoing Ipgrave's design) are teachers exhorting students to recognize first that religions, as a facet of diversity, are intrinsically valuable; second that appreciation of them, even despite not agreeing with them, is a good end in itself; and third that the overarching aim is to contribute to the common good (however the teacher defines that). This, of course, is an example of liberal universalism. What it does not do is fully get to grips with the nature of religion and its different forms, especially some of those forms mentioned in earlier chapters. Equally, Jackson's use of the phrase 'within the law' is open to presuming that religious forms that challenge democratic rights are not 'within the law' (presuming law here to mean democratically instituted law). Therefore, a question remains as to how law defined by other nation states (for example religious ones, as with the interpretation of Sharia law that operates in Iran) is to be viewed, especially in relation to Islamic blasphemy laws and penalties imposed (which also pertain to Afghanistan and Pakistan). Similarly we can note laws against homosexuality in certain African states. Surely, 'within the law' acts as a restrictive and somewhat ambiguous imposition on the study of religion. If we use the UN Charter of Human Rights as our standard, we have already noted in Chapter 1 the ambiguities that can apply to this. Whilst Jackson is at pains within the numerous practical research examples he gives to show that the agency of children is at the forefront of this approach,[8] nevertheless these reports all record a movement toward the overarching disposition of valuing diversity without questioning its value. It seems strange for an educational enquiry based on a dialogic model to state, at the outset, that diversity (presumably of any kind) is to be valued as a guiding premise of the enquiry and the dialogue. Surely, this is not only educationally unjustifiable but also somewhat undemocratic. It is pertinent to ask, if the good of some states of affairs is to be taken as an unquestioned given, should that not lead us to question them as a means to testing their value, on principle, within a democratic form of education in a democratic society?

The lack of critical enquiry into diversity has also resulted in a positive representation of ethnic minority groups and religions. Thus they tend to be idealized and often presented as victims of inequality. As Trevor Phillips, Chair of the Equality and Human Rights Commission, wrote:

> Our ideal should be one nation of many faces; one culture integrating many faiths and traditions. But how we get there is contentious. ... I remarked last month that it was time for Britain to move on from divisive, 80s-style 'multiculturalist' policies. ... Integration only works if it both recognizes newcomers' differences and extends complete equality. Celebrating diversity, but ignoring inequality, inevitably leads to the nightmare of entrenched segregation. ... And yes, newcomers do have to change. The language barrier is a real obstacle to work, friendship and democratic participation. ... But we have to do more than teach people English. Too many institutions have seized one half of the integration equation – recognition of difference – while ignoring the other half: equality.[9]

Whilst Phillips has a point in terms of multiculturalism's lack of incisiveness in not highlighting the need for equality there is also a need to identify whether 'newcomers' themselves share this same concern for equality within their own communities. As an example we can cite the article in the *Observer* newspaper by Nick Cohen, 'The secret scandal of Britain's caste system'.[10] Cohen notes that:

> British Asians, secularists and Liberal Democrat and Labour politicians have been trying for years to persuade the government to tackle caste discrimination. They have had no success because the treatment of untouchables is one of the great unmentionables of British politics. They are certainly the victims of a form of religious prejudice. ... Yet caste

prejudice does not fit easily into established views on how discrimination works.

Cohen makes reference to a study conducted by the National Institute of Economic and Social Research in which, to quote one of many examples, 'The Indian supervisor of an NHS worker discovers he is from a lower caste and makes his life such a misery he becomes ill under the pressure and is suspended.'

Cohen lays a large portion of blame at the door of Trevor Phillips as Chair of the Equality and Human Rights Commission and, in searching their website, notes that it 'ignores caste discrimination in Britain'. He concludes,

> I can only guess that Phillips does not like admitting that ethnic minorities as well as white people are capable of prejudice. He may worry, too, that an honest stance would require him taking on religious lobbyists, such as the Hindu Council UK, which questioned 'the existence of caste discrimination in the UK' and claimed that the issue was being manipulated by Christians eager to convert Hindus from their faith.[11]

And the problem runs deeper, as honour killings, genital mutilation, the treatment of women and attitudes toward homosexuals amongst sections of minority groups are all well documented. But multiculturalism and anti-racism have, again in Cohen's words, 'promoted minority group rights – the rights of blocks of immigrants not to be penalized for their colour or creed – rather than the rights of individuals not to be persecuted by their own "community"'.[12]

It is this double standard, highlighted by Cohen, that should lead us to question the way in which diversity is represented in religious education. It lacks any critical incisiveness, it could justifiably be claimed that it does not provide a balanced view, and therefore the problematizing of it is both necessary and overdue. A fundamental issue that Cohen draws attention to is the tension between the twin principles of liberalism, the right to free speech on the one hand (based on freedom of conscience), which allows for criticism and even offence, and tolerance on the other. The tolerance principle is the one that has been promoted at the same time as the free speech principle has been demoted. Thus, there has been plenty of criticism of and lack of support for individuals who have fallen foul of intolerant voices and groups within religions. Notable individuals to whom this has happened are Salman Rushdie, Ayaan Hirsi Ali and Theo Van Gogh, but there have been many more. Despite the intended and actual violence toward these individuals, perpetrated by religious groups, comparatively little support has been offered for the right of free speech to the victims. Cohen remarks, 'If the historians of the future have one ounce of morality, they will damn the European left for its inability to oppose racism and support individual liberty simultaneously.'[13]

Equally, while religious education has promoted the tolerance principle, often raising it to the level of respect for all religions, it has, comparatively, neglected the free speech principle. This is why it has had to contend, as a result, that militant religious groups are not really the true face of religion and nor are those groups who abuse human, women's and children's rights, because if they were recognized as simply a different expression of many-faceted religious forms (infused, as all religion is, with differing social, cultural and political characteristics) then the tolerance argument is undermined.

RE and textual interpretation

Apologetic and progressive readings of religious texts are another case of defending religion against negative criticism. They most often amount to pointing out that what the text literally says was not its intention. An example of this is *Reading the Qur'an* by Ziaddin Sardar. In her review of this, Malise Ruthven identifies how he deals with controversial verses. As one example she cites the:

> seemingly patronizing or misogynistic passage stating that the testimony of one man is worth that of two women in certain legal proceedings – a rubric that has made it virtually impossible for a woman in some Muslim countries to bring an accusation of rape against a man without herself incurring a charge of *zina* or sexual misconduct. Sardar argues that where the specific conditions that determined the circumstances of this revelation – a higher rate of illiteracy or innumeracy among females rather than males – have changed the requirement no longer need apply. All that the Qur'an is suggesting is 'that different situations require different kinds of witnesses'.[14]

This is, of course, preposterous given the sacred status of the Qur'an for Muslims and the claim that the text is inerrant and eternal. Whilst one can sympathize with a reading, or rather an interpretation that makes it more fit for modern times, this is simply not what the Qur'an says and, therefore, not what is practised. What we are witnessing is a Western liberal applauding an interpretation of the text that fits with Western liberalism. It sets a precedent for others to devise a different interpretation compatible with their own worldview and moral sensitivities. If one complained that this has always been the case, then there is no case for making any text sacred as it stands, which, of course, becomes an affront to most believers. What this interpretation also does, of course, is reveal the pre-modern value systems of many believers. Only when that is problematized do we get at the significant issues concerning this interpretation of the purposes of RE that I have highlighted above.

There is a hermeneutical corruption in Sadar's interpretation of the Qur'anic verses. He seeks to give them an interpretation in line with Western liberalism. But what he is actually doing is making the unpalatable palatable. The hermeneutic agent is liberalism itself. What is so wearying about this device is that it seeks to preserve the authority of the text in the context of liberalism. It does not allow the text to be rendered obsolete and deficient. This, ironically, is the same device used by fundamentalists to ensure that the meaning of the text can be changed so that the text can never be wrong.[15] The hermeneutical rules for determining the meaning are changed to ensure this is so, in both the liberal and fundamentalist case. James Barr speaks of the fundamentalist desire to 'preserve [the meaning of the text] rather than rebuild'.[16] This is, of course, the reverse of the liberalizing process, which is to construct a progressive interpretation. It is a classic instance of pre-modernist and modernist readings of scriptural texts but the significant thing is that neither is rooted in the authority of scripture per se but in the authority of conservatism or liberalism respectively. The scriptural text retains its authority perversely, by acknowledgement of the hermeneutical agency (whether conservative or liberal). The meaning of the text is, therefore, relative.

However, even those willing to admit that the holy text is relative to time and place, and can be outmoded, still wish to preserve its authority. The following argument is indicative of a habit of mind quite widespread in religious liberals and liberal RE. This example is provided by Jonathan Romain but it is simply indicative of the way in which liberal apologists still wish to maintain the privileged and protected status of religious texts. Jonathan Romain, the Rabbi of Maidenhead synagogue, is willing to admit that:

> the declaration of 'an eye for eye, tooth for tooth' in Exodus 21:24 ... is totally inappropriate today. ... The rabbis of previous centuries also realized the verse was both unworkable and immoral. However, they felt unable to alter the text itself. ... Their solution was to interpret away the surface meaning. ... However, the unpalatable text of Exodus is still in place ... and the verse has become a theological albatross around Jewish necks.[17]

As a result, he quotes the tenth-century Jewish scholar Saadiah Gaon saying 'The main causes of irreligion are the weak and ridiculous arguments advanced in defence of faith.'[18] Nevertheless, Romain concludes that, 'So whereas in the days of King James believers would have felt obliged to justify every verse, we can be more honest and more relaxed: not denying its weaknesses and thereby not tarnishing its strengths.'[19]

The position Romain has put himself in, though he does not and would not declare it, is to place the Jewish Bible or any other sacred scripture, if we were to extend his argument and judgement, on the same level as any other literature in which we might find wisdom but also flaws. It is no longer inerrant and therefore (presumably) cannot be regarded as sacred because it is no longer a revelation from a perfect source. As a result it should be judged by its inherent worth, not by the infallible authority from which it purportedly comes and which it reflects. It is to be judged relative to the value of other works of literature and other chronicles. It is not surprising that irreligion proceeds from weak arguments in defence of faith but, more importantly, irreligion is justified by these defences and Romain does not help his religious cause with such a disingenuous defence as is offered here. I wish to make clear that this is not an attack on Romain as such but on the much more widespread position that liberals often hold as a form of textual rearguard apologetics to protect the idea of sacred texts when the basis for their sacredness has been eroded. They fail to take that last logical step that their analysis implies.

If students in the RE classroom are to become theologically and politically literate, the debate over the meanings and value of religious texts, rehearsed in outline above, needs to be a central aspect of the RE curriculum. This is not because it is important to know the crucial texts or to be morally inspired by them and recognize their worth and authority, but because it is an important exercise in hermeneutics that gives students the capacity to make informed judgements on them.

RE as an investigation into truth claims

Whilst for socio-anthropologically, ethnographically and phenomenologically based approaches to RE truth is an empirical exercise based on the representation of religion, for others truth is about metaphysical matters, notably in the writings of Andrew Wright with his critical realist stance.[20] Here the idea is that one can discern the veracity of various religions' claims to truth by subjecting them to critical scrutiny. The problems in this endeavour are manifold. There is a serious problem in the way in which quests for meaning are translated into claims of truth. At the heart of this are also claims to knowledge. These three terms, meaning, truth and knowledge, tend to be used interchangeably or, without justification, be transmuted from the one to the other. For example, a religious truth claim is also justified as a claim to knowledge but it is difficult to understand on what basis, apart from revelation, that it is anything more than a way of constructing meaning. Does a claim to revelation provide the requisite justification for a claim to truth or knowledge? More difficult still are the justifications and premises provided for both knowledge and truth, which bear no similarity to scientific claims for justifying the same concepts. Whilst claiming otherwise, religious claims to knowledge and truth reduce their status to 'subjective truth' paraded as 'objective truth' on the basis of the connection made between personal experience and divine revelation. Also, those who invest in the justification of metaphysics are most often interested parties. For example, Wright's approach is influenced by his own Christian beliefs in the truth of Trinitarian Christianity and its dogmas. This makes his enquiry into religious truths also somewhat compromised even if the approach to religious education he espouses does not explicitly base its outcome upon his own confessional position. Even so,

Wright adds that we can learn 'virtues of wisdom and the pursuit of truth' without any necessary prior commitment to any particular 'foundational meta-narrative', be it critical realism or any other.[21]

A further problem ensues when one is aware that no religious claim to truth is in any way verifiable or falsifiable because there are no bases on which this could be judged. All natural laws are suspended in this fanciful land in which everything is possible if you can claim it happened and there is sufficient support for such a claim from believers. And this is the rub. Whatever is sufficiently supported has to be accepted in the public domain. A rule by consensus. That takes us no nearer to the question of truth but much further in the direction of relativism – which everyone with vested interests in this game seeks to deny at all costs because then they all lose: claims to truth have no purchase outside those who are already believers, and others' claims to truth necessarily have equal status. But now claims to truth are no more than assertions of meaning-making. In effect this means that religious claims to truth can be justified by any manner of means in the popular imagination: miracles, rational argument unsupported by empirical investigation that rests upon premises that are always contestable (such as arguments for the existence of God), claims that certain religions have a greater claim to rational or revelatory truth than others. But all these arguments eschew the need for a more rigorous investigation.

In his book Critical Religious Education, Multiculturalism and the Pursuit of Truth,[22] Andrew Wright quotes Douglas Popora favourably. Popora states that: 'We so lack any articulated worldview that arguments about the cosmos strike us as ponderously irrelevant. Today we shy away from thinking cosmically.'[23]

Following this, Wright links Popora's comment on thinking cosmically to the way in which we find moral purpose. He comments that 'our social relationships require a moral perspective to give them meaning,' and quotes Popora saying that 'Just as moral space is where we find moral purpose', so 'moral purpose must be emotionally and conceptually grounded in some larger worldview.'[24] Wright then adds that because worldviews make claims about what is, they ineluctably raise questions of truth, questions that 'move us into the space of critical argument' and that Popora's research reveals 'a culturally pervasive lack of orientation in metaphysical space, an inability to place ourselves meaningfully in the cosmos', which leads to 'an equally pervasive void in our sense of self. ... we cannot lose our place in the cosmos without losing ourselves as well.'[25] Wright concludes:

> Whether implicitly or explicitly, we cannot avoid acting in social and moral space without some assumptions about metaphysical space [and] our ability to attend to questions of our place in the cosmos has been severely retarded by the forces of secularization that strive to remove such questions from the public sphere.[26]

This is a curious argument. Reconstructing it so that it gives a better understanding of what exactly is being argued reveals why. First, Wright says we must have some assumptions about metaphysical space. Second, this can be related to why we need to advance critical argument. Third, without a sense of the metaphysical order of things we are disorientated. Fourth, as a result, we have no moral purpose. Fifth, we therefore lose our sense of self. Sixth, our capacity to attend to questions that orient ourselves in the cosmos is retarded by secularization.

In effect, what this argument advances is that:

1   Without a religious metaphysical construction of the cosmos (presumably including our existential understanding of ourselves within that) we lack the capacity to understand ourselves or our world.
2   The construction of such a metaphysical map, based on assumptions about truth, gives us a sense of self and world that can be critically argued.
3   This construction of such a map gives us moral purpose, a sense of truth and a sense of meaning.
4   Secularization retards this capacity on a personal, cultural and social level.

Thus, without a metaphysical worldview we become impoverished, disorientated, even retarded morally. Also, since secularized thought cannot provide such a worldview, that worldview, and metaphysic, must be religious. We may notice that 'truth' within this argument is based on assumptions that are to be critically analysed. But how do you analyse an assumption? Only by questioning its premises, logic and supporting evidence. It is in the nature of many aspects of religious worldviews that they cannot be fully analysed in this way because of the supra-mundane nature of their claims. Therefore, truth can mean no more than assumption (i.e. believing in something because it is said to be true, or believing because it is claimed as a revelation, or being persuaded by it because we subjectively feel it speaks to our personal condition).[27] Significantly, the argument posits that the main outcome of such an exercise is to give us a sense of meaning and moral purpose. Thus, it can be concluded that a secular 'worldview' does not provide these capacities; it leads to a meaningless and amoral world.

This analysis reveals the intentions behind Wright's position, which is to say that without religion we are without direction, orientation and morality. It would therefore follow that without a curriculum subject called religious education that provides for a critical discussion of metaphysical (religious) worldviews young people will grow up aimless, alienated and without moral purpose.

Disguised within this argument is the idea that only religions can make truth claims. As a result, we can conclude that such truth claims are based on assumptions that defy rational explanation or the possibility of empirical foundation. Therefore, what value is there in proposing critical analysis, especially if secular alternative viewpoints are to be ignored? It would appear that behind this proposal of RE as an investigation into truth claims is a nurturing intent that presents religious worldviews as the only vehicles to create moral persons.

Beyond this we can criticize Wright's position on the basis that it operates within a particular 'knowledge' paradigm (for further comment on this see Chapter 9). In this paradigm terms like truth, reality and (as Wright has also claimed) objectivity are not based on the same principles as those used in the natural and social sciences, where empirical observations are the basis of such claims. In this paradigm these terms relate to a defence of belief through the use of rationality. I have no problem with the defence of belief, but there is a need to identify the paradigmatic difference on which its claims are made (largely rhetorical in the sense of seeking to be persuasive) and to recognize that this form of 'knowledge' and its usages of terms such as 'truth' depend upon an acceptance of the paradigm in which they are contextualized.

Wright effectively becomes the inheritor of his theological forebears in RE, except that his confessionality is enlarged from defending Christianity to defending religion. His introduction of a critical perspective is not so much a case of introducing openness into religious education as of intending that, for students, RE should amount to a particular form of theological nurturing through a form of critical inter-faith dialogue.

The important distinction that must be pursued is the basis upon which truth claims are made. They can claim to be subjective or objective, but it is difficult to understand how religious claims could be the latter. They are either pursued on the basis of subjective understanding (by an individual) or on the basis of agreement by a representative body (the Vatican Council or a similar body in other churches or religions) which then proceeds to enshrine them in doctrines. This subjectivist process ensures that the power and influence of religions is also present in religious education. Its influence is seen in the religious presence on Standing Advisory Councils on RE (SACREs), discussed by Mark in Chapter 6.

Representation therefore ignores the ways in which religion is or has been detrimental and focuses on its positivity. It is taken for granted that religions are rational. Also, since the representatives of religions on SACREs belong to particular branches of a religion, its representation will reflect that. Thus, as a result, particular negative impressions of religion will be erased from the curriculum: paedophile Roman Catholic priests, forced marriages in Islam or honour killings, caste injustices and the like will be put down to tribal, societal and cultural norms, and seen as unfortunate occurrences that have nothing to do with the religion in question. Clearly, therefore, religion has little influence on societal, cultural or moral behaviour. The problem lies elsewhere. Unless, that is, it can claim credit for any form of moral rectitude; which it does by pointing the finger at secularism and materialism as the cause of ills in a Godless or religionless society.

Therefore there are three major problems with approaching RE as an enquiry into truth claims. The first is that the truth criteria are hopelessly confused; the second is that the truth criteria are based on belief; and the third is that this approach does not pay attention to religion on the ground or the messiness of religion being caught up in societies and politics.

Conclusion

In all three approaches to RE presented above we do however notice particular similarities. The first is the positive protection of religion in its representation and the respectability of its claims. Following on from that, the second is the lack of scrutiny given to the rational incoherence and unacceptable practices of some religious forms. We may presume that both these failures are due to the desire to ensure that religion retains an acceptable face within modern democratic ways of life, and that the purposes of RE fall in line with that desire. In Chapter 6 we see how this favouring of specific religious interests is embedded in the political structures that underpin RE in its English context.

Response from Mark Chater

In a time of deregulation and debate, it is likely that we will see an increase in diversification and innovation for RE. It is possible that the theoretical models discussed here by Clive (and by others) will find their way into practical approaches. This is to be welcomed in so far as it brings theorists and practitioners into closer proximity, increasing the accountability of the former and enhancing the rigour and critical perspective to the latter. However, RE still needs safeguards that prevent particular local authorities or schools from becoming, in effect, laboratories of any approach that might catch the eye.

RE has a celebrated capacity for self-reinvention, which it has used to great effect over the decades since anthropological and phenomenological models first gained their hegemony. In some ways, however, self-reinvention has been skin-deep, while the long-term project of RE, to give sympathetic representation to religion and religions, has continued under the surface. For example, critical interpretation in a dialogical setting can only operate if groundwork has been completed, addressing questions of why all parties should address diversity and difference. If an approach takes it for granted that attending to religious and other viewpoints through dialogue must be self-evidently worthwhile, there will be some learners whose behaviour, demeanour or reasoning will put this unspoken assumption to the test. Similarly, in seeking to open up 'questions of ultimate truth'[28] or to promote understanding of 'the ultimate order-of-things',[29] RE invites, or perhaps incites, some learners to respond by questioning the assumption of ultimacy. Practitioners must judge whether these constructions, and others, are offering a transformational difference, or whether they are a continuation of the strategy of adaptation and positive representation.

But if it would be a mistake for RE practitioners to clutch blindly at any proffered rationale in hope of a complete answer, it would be equally unwise to conclude that the search for a justifiable rationale is fruitless – that RE is condemned to wander the educational desert, homeless and defenceless. That condition, as many religious and philosophical narratives suggest, is not for ever, and is usually resolved through a crisis.

Chapter 6

The politics of English RE
A portrait of disfunctionality

Mark Chater

Opening Story

Standing Advisory Councils on Religious Education and their impact on English RE: a tale of two SACREs

Story 1

2 p.m. in the social wing of a gurdwara. At the reception desk, two young Sikh adults are there to greet members, hand them a badge and papers, and show them to the meeting room. Refreshments and music are part of the atmosphere as people gather and greet each other. The SACRE has a full membership of 30, and nearly all have indicated their intention to be present. The clerk, adviser and chair have met earlier in the day to discuss how the business should be conducted.

The first item is a film clip of young people and their teachers talking about RE. Prompted by questions, the young people speak their mind about RE, praising the fact that it gives them a look at the wider world and enables them to think and speak for themselves. They also criticize some aspects of whole-class teaching and the examination course. The teachers on the film share their perspectives about how they feel RE contributes to young people's thinking skills. After the film, SACRE members are asked to discuss its points in small groups, and come up with proposals for building on the strengths and addressing the weaknesses.

The next item is a report from the Adviser, outlining how some of the strengths and weaknesses compare with national findings, and suggesting some practical projects, including an initiative to meet the local authority's assessment adviser, a collaboration with neighbouring SACREs and online collaboration with SACREs in similar parts of the country.

After an hour and a half, and several other business items, the meeting breaks up and people leave, feeling proud and excited that their voluntary work is making a difference to young people.

Story 2

6 p.m. in an echoing school hall. Trestle tables are laid out for ten; six people have arrived, and the chair is worried that the meeting might not be quorate. With a few seconds to spare, a seventh member bustles in with apologies; the meeting now has a quorum and can begin. A prayer is said.

Under matters arising, the secretary reports on further correspondence from a local member of the British Humanist Association, who wishes to become a member of the SACRE. The letter argues that, as non-religious worldviews can be a part of RE, the SACRE might benefit from some humanist input. The meeting decides to decline this suggestion because, as one member puts it, 'this is a religious subject.'

The main item is to discuss a review of the local agreed syllabus. The chair regretfully announces that there has been no response to requests for a budget. As the local authority has no adviser, correspondence has been slow. The sole councillor present is not from the ruling party, and can offer little practical advice or help in persuading decision makers. She promises to raise it at the next education committee, which meets in three weeks' time. The matter is deferred until the next SACRE meeting.

A representative from one of the religions expresses the hope that the next syllabus will give more time to his religion, which he feels is under-represented in the present syllabus compared with some others. This is noted by the secretary. Some members quietly wonder whether this request is appropriate, but they do not wish to seem impolite by questioning it, so there is no discussion.

One member asks what RE is doing to make young people behave better. He complains of the atmosphere of disrespect among young people in the shops and on the streets, and wants to know why RE isn't doing a better job of teaching young people the difference between right and wrong. This provokes a heated argument about social mores and the purpose of RE. No one is able to report authoritatively on what the local syllabus says about moral issues, or how effective it is.

Two hours later, the meeting breaks up. The chair feels uncomfortable and upset about the disagreement. Other members leave feeling a little gloomy and frustrated, but not knowing what they can do to move things forward.

A critical introduction

Standing Advisory Councils on Religious Education (SACREs) exist by law in every local authority in England and Wales. They have existed since before the 1944 Education Act, and they became mandatory for each local authority in the 1988 Education Reform Act. Their existence and purpose has been reaffirmed in subsequent legislation[1] in terms of promoting RE and forming a link between the local authority and those concerned with RE. The existence of SACREs places legal obligations on local authorities in England and Wales, whose duties include establishing a SACRE with a specified structure, establishing an occasional agreed syllabus conference, reviewing the agreed syllabus every five years, and other duties relevant to representation on the SACRE.[2]

The functions and duties of SACREs consist of a legal minimum of reporting tasks and a set of responsibilities that are considered good practice but not required by law. For example, SACREs are legally required to publish an annual report, but their activity in monitoring the quality of RE in schools – something one would have thought necessary in order to compile a meaningful report – is not legally required, and is defined in non-statutory guidance.[3] Similarly, the offering of advice on effective teaching, and on interpreting the agreed syllabus, is a non-statutory activity, considered good practice but not legally required.[4] The balance of statutory to non-statutory expectations in relation to SACREs is problematic: the total number of legal requirements on LAs, SACREs and SACRE sub-committees is 15 legal 'musts' to nine non-statutory 'shoulds' or 'mays'.[5] Furthermore, those activities that are likely to impact most directly on the classroom quality of the subject, teachers' understanding of their pedagogy, and public understanding of the place of RE – such as offering advice, taking care in the design and balance of syllabuses, visiting schools, creating partnerships or contributing to inter-faith and community relations – are all matters of non-statutory choice, not absolute requirements.[6] Thus there is a built-in tendency for SACREs, and those in local authorities who manage or service them, to think bureaucratically first, and only then to have regard for points of good practice. This has produced, over the decades, a compliance mentality in which SACREs have expected to comply, and to be complied with, in ways that no longer work in a changing school system. It is true that in normal times, good practice as defined in non-statutory guidance has usually carried an authority almost equal to the law; this has meant that the 'shoulds', 'mays', case studies and checklists of the 2010 guidance would normally be highly influential across local authorities. But the sequence of thinking first about legal requirements and subsequently about good practice has nevertheless corroded the creativity of SACREs, and this problem has been very considerably exacerbated in the local authority cutbacks from 2009–10 onwards. It is commonplace for local authorities, under pressure to make painful budgetary decisions, to consider only what they must do and to abandon what they should or may do. Even the 'musts' can disappear unless sufficient pressure is exerted to protect them.

The composition of SACREs is laid down by law in the form of four groups. These four represent some of the different sections of interest in RE:

- group A: Christian denominations and such other religions and religious denominations as, in the authority's opinion, will appropriately reflect the principal religious traditions in the area;
- group B: the Church of England;
- group C: teacher associations;
- group D: the local authority.[7]

Four corresponding committees compose the agreed syllabus conference, which is charged with developing an agreed syllabus for RE. Group A varies in range of membership, depending on the demographics of the local authority. In practice, nearly all SACREs recognize that they are educating young people for life not solely within their administrative boundary but in a globalized world, and that their RE should reflect at least the full range of six principal religions. An increasing number of SACREs have wanted to go further, by including other religions and non-religious worldviews, as recommended in the 2004 framework.[8] However, disparities occur: while authorities in London, Manchester, Birmingham or other areas find little difficulty in accessing the full range, more rural authorities still aspire to include the full range but, since their population tends to be less religiously diverse, find this challenging or impossible to achieve. More seriously, many SACREs have felt it inappropriate to include humanists on group A, even if they include humanism in their syllabus. One major humanist membership organization, the British Humanist Association, was a signatory to the 2004 framework and its successor documents in 2007 and 2010. The BHA remains an active though critical supporter of this inclusive model of RE. Several SACREs co-opt humanists, but this falls short of having full membership as of right. Some claim that it would be wrong to include humanists because the subject is called religious education. Others believe it would be an illegal step to include this group, while others argue that it is illegal not to. These claims have never been tested in English courts, and the government has not given an authoritative interpretation of the law on this point. This unresolved issue creates confusion and division in each SACRE where the problem is raised.

In respect of group A, SACRE membership operates more by use and custom than by clear principles. The structure of all four groups, seen through the prism of equal opportunity and partnership, is arbitrary, restrictive and old-fashioned.

SACRE structures and their impact on RE

The RE community has debated the role of SACREs widely since 1988. However, there has been limited critical discussion of the structure of membership and the ways in which this structure influences the quality and integrity of RE. The structure of four goups owes its genesis to an era in which England was less diverse, and less aware of its diversity: this accounts for the prioritization of the Church of England in group B, and the use of phrases such as 'other religions', which feels less inclusive and less respectful now. It may also account for the static sense that representation must be through official channels, for example teacher associations; there are more fluid and open ways of representing teachers available in our time. The problem that often presents itself in SACREs now is that the static and dated forms of structure in the four groups have a backward influence on the character of representation.

The fact that two of the four groups are made up of practising members of religious communities, while only one represents teachers, creates an imbalance between the religious and the educational forces acting on RE. The fact that, in many SACREs, finding active members is challenging leads to an ethos of volunteerism in which almost any willing member is welcomed, even if their understanding of RE, or of the doctrine and practice of their religion, is incomplete or partial. Several SACREs operate a semi-confidential system of vetting before admitting anyone to membership; in many ways this is a sensible precaution, even though it is open to accusations of lacking democratic transparency. Even such a precaution does not always succeed in protecting SACREs from accepting members with hobby horses or with less than ideal qualifications to be in control of RE. The notion that a local leading member of a faith is qualified to represent that faith in its full complexity, subtlety and internal diversity, and to participate in curriculum design and decisions, has proved troublesome in a number of SACREs, and rarely works well unless the SACRE is led by an adviser or consultant who carries strong counterweight credibility as an educationalist. There is no test for SACRE membership, and even if there were, it would be hard to judge whether a potential member of group A or B were capable of distinguishing between his/her own theological preferences and the range of positions adopted in his/her faith tradition nationally and globally. A competent SACRE member has a moral duty to make this distinction constantly, and apply it to a range of theological, moral and cultural differences. Beyond this task, there is also the higher duty to collaborate in constructing RE proposals that are educationally appropriate for children and young people. To require this of volunteers, some of whom have never thought educationally about their own beliefs, is supremely challenging: little wonder that it does not often work. Advisers and experienced SACRE members have observed that it is helpful, and healthy, to draw religious leaders into an educational milieu where they are challenged to begin thinking critically and educationally: that such thinking is virtuous, and can help religious communities to be more open. This is a position that we will consider more deeply in Chapter 8, when we discuss the educational economy of religions. But the voluntary nature of the arrangements makes any quality assurance on religious input and advice virtually impossible, and this creates, in the RE system, a series of anomalies and susceptibilities that begin in SACRE structures and end in weakening the whole of RE.

The weaknesses in this structure carry through to agreed syllabuses and, therefore, to the quality of learning in classrooms. First, the built-in religious majority ensures that religious content will be packaged and offered in particular ways. Religious representatives will be motivated to ensure that their religion gains and keeps adequate amounts of time in the syllabus: from this concern comes a default way of designing syllabuses, based around content, that looks increasingly antiquated and unconvincing as learning. The idea that learning can be concerned with religion or belief in itself, its nature and impact, rather than confined to separate religions or beliefs, quite often fails to prevail in syllabus design; the idea that learning might examine religions or beliefs critically, explore their internal divisions and debates, expose their less tolerant facets to young people's gaze, or garner young people's suggestions on how to improve the contribution of religions and beliefs, often has to be fought for and does not always succeed against the interests of the religious representatives. The commonly held notions that RE should 'cover' a range of religions, and that RE should combat secularization, together with the common practice of attempting to represent those religions positively in classrooms, all are educationally questionable, and all owe a great deal to the inbuilt religious majority in the group structure of SACREs and agreed syllabus conferences.

The presence of teacher and council representation (through Groups C and D) can also bring weaknesses that carry through to the quality of RE. If given a free hand and asked for an honest answer, most teachers and teacher representatives would opt for a minimum-change syllabus at each review. Professional self-interest, and the widely shared feeling that there is already too much change in the system, make this nearly inevitable. Unless strongly led by an adviser, or unusually led by a teacher with a Master's-level understanding of curriculum and pedagogy, teacher representatives tend to lack awareness of how they can shape learning, and they lack the time to pay close attention to national developments – for example, in curriculum aims, or learning strategies – that should shape the context of their work. Where SACREs could be offering a free flow of ideas between national policy developments, research insights and practitioner perspectives, too often the teacher representation tends to advocate a conservative approach, minimizing change and filtering out wider factors. Local authority representatives want to keep costs down, and this, too, often leans towards minimum-change solutions. They want a syllabus that bolsters municipal identity and pride, and they recognize that this must be based on consensus.

Despite these susceptibilities, there are some excellent agreed syllabuses in use, characterized by inventive, engaging enquiries into the natures of religion and belief, and into combinations of religions, single religions or philosophical issues. It is nearly always true that such syllabuses are created because of the skilled leadership of an adviser or consultant. There are also many less good syllabuses, where the structure inside the units has become too complex or idiosyncratic to be coherent, and a few very dated ones, unaffected by curricular or pedagogical thinking over a ten-year period.

Two particular characteristics of nearly all agreed syllabuses add to their weakness as curriculum tools. The first is their tendency is to give RE four, five or six aims as a subject, aims which are unrelated to the overall aims of the curriculum. This emphasizes the complexity, internal contradictions and isolation of the subject. It exposes a vulnerability in RE, namely that it is an uneasy coalition of several disciplines – theology, religious studies, sociology, biblical studies, ethics, to name some – and as such does not have a coherent, strong identity as a discipline in its own right. Second, nearly all syllabuses use the two attainment targets inherited from the 2004 framework, learning about religion and learning from religion. The inherently confused nature of these two targets has been discussed in Chapter 3. The confusion is deepened, however, by the practice of divorcing the two targets from definitions of progress and attainment. Thus it has been common for many syllabuses to adopt the 2004 framework's eight-level scale, with its six strands, but to offer a range of content and units bearing no relation to the strands of the scale. The result is skewed: one thing is taught, but another is assessed. School inspectors have observed, with concern, that this confuses planning and depresses standards in RE.[9] These two characteristics have a negative impact on teachers' understanding of their task in RE, on planning and on definitions of attainment.

The legal duty to produce an agreed syllabus acts as an invisible force on SACREs, making them emphasize reaching agreement, rather than producing a document that has coherence or educational strength. RE inspectors have commented on how over-complex and incoherent structures in several agreed syllabuses – the result of competing religious and educational priorities – have tended to produce muddled planning and only satisfactory teaching in several schools.[10]

Schools use SACREs and agreed syllabuses in different ways. Where a secondary head of RE is confident, knowledgeable and has a good grasp of the subject overall, it is quite common for there to be only a loose, occasional reference to the agreed syllabus. Where there is less confidence, there is more reliance on the syllabus. In primary schools, teachers must learn to use a syllabus that is almost always laid out differently from the national curriculum documents of all other subjects, and this can prove a considerable obstacle to coherent planning. Some primary teachers report anxiety in relation to teaching RE: particularly recurrent fears are that by getting some aspect of content wrong, they might cause offence, that they do not feel equal to dealing with ultimate questions and do not know how to handle their own beliefs.[11] The anxiety can sometimes feed on a more generalized, unspoken unease about RE, usually based on a weak understanding of its educational rationale and aims. In primary schools, increasing numbers of teachers deal with this general unease and specific anxiety by adopting a number of evasive strategies, including handing over RE to a teaching assistant, teaching didactically and sticking mainly with 'learning about' approaches.

The four-group structure is also deficient in omitting several constituencies now recognized as having interests and rights in RE that hold equal moral legitimacy to those who are currently represented. For example, employers, university academics in philosophy, theology, religious studies or teacher education, school leaders, governors and parents, and pupils themselves, are all excluded by the present structure. There have been enterprising SACREs that have reached out to several of these constituencies and used co-option to include them. The power structure is engineered against them: they may be included, but they have no place as of right, and cannot vote. Yet each of these groups could, in different ways, enrich the potential of RE to offer learning of high quality, and promote better public understanding of the subject.

For the era in which the four-group structure was devised – pre-digital, culturally static and municipally corporatist – SACREs served well enough as forums of a liberal consensus around a content-led model of RE. However, none of those conditions pertain now, and the fluidity of structural thinking leaves SACREs behind. Contemporary curriculum design recognizes the better alternatives to a content-led approach, for example through the five competencies of the RSA Opening Minds curriculum,[12] in which content is chosen with pupils involved. In such contexts, at least the contested discourse about what should be in the curriculum is conducted openly, and includes a wide range of stakeholders. But little of such open contestation happens in SACREs, because of their fixed and closed structures. We must now face the evidence that SACREs in their present structural form are mufflers and blocks more often than not. They muffle learning by prioritizing the interests of religious groups, privileging certain communities and excluding others. They block change by allying the sectional conservatism of teachers and the financial interests of councils. They lack a remit to shape pedagogy, and are inhibited from proffering any definition of knowledge, skill or understanding that does not accord with the religious, professional and financial agendas of those who must reach agreement.

SACREs and the curriculum: an analogy

The inadequate and unjust nature of this structure, and its negative impact on teaching and learning, might be helpfully conceived if we were to imagine a comparable structure for another curriculum subject. Let us suppose, then, that Design and Technology is locally determined, and that legal responsibility for the local D&T curriculum is placed in the hands of local bodies – called SACDATs – composed with a similar structure. Committees A and B are representatives of producer bodies, C of teachers and D of local authority health and safety experts. Committee A is allowed representation from B&Q, Do-it-all, Argos and Ikea. However, the federation of independent ironmongers, the building trade and freelance carpenters are not included, despite their request. Committee B may include Tesco, Sainsbury's, Asda and Waitrose, but not dairy farmers, wholefood outlets, vegetarian networks or fairtrade retailers. Committees A and B establish a consensus on the range of products that can appear in classrooms. On Committee C, teachers find the uniformity convenient. Local authority health and safety interests, expressed through Committee D, can be inexpensively reduced to accepting that the product-led approach driven by Committees A and B comes with national standards of health and safety built in, making expensive local checking mechanisms unnecessary. They also like the way that the big chains present themselves as 'your local store', underpinning an appropriate sense of local community pride.

Let us further imagine that representatives from several environmental groups are concerned about what they see as the unimaginative teaching of D&T in schools, and they seek representation on the local SACDAT in order to influence change. The groups vary from those who seek to make young people more aware of their carbon footprint and those who want to encourage schools to grow more of their own food, to those who want to promote young people's practical skills. In their different ways, each of these groups could significantly challenge the consensus pedagogy of the subject, by introducing new questions about design and by exposing ethical issues about some products. The producer committees are quick to reject this approach, arguing that the new organizations are not legitimate players in the world of design or technology – and darkly suggesting that some of them may not have children's best interests at heart. While a few teachers recognize that the new organizations could offer an interesting development for their subject, the majority do not want the disturbance to their chosen methodology.

Most SACDATs reject the approach of new would-be members and decline to address issues of pedagogy. Over time, D&T continues to be taught in the same way. The consensus survives.

But in the real world, SACREs have no equivalent in any other subject: a fact which forces them into a position as *sui generis* adjuncts to an educational structure that often knows little about them. Local authorities, unless prompted by a strong and articulate adviser, may often be blind to the potential of their local SACRE and may, for example, miss opportunities to connect a SACRE's remit with local community cohesion efforts or skills promotion work. Similarly the public knows very little about SACREs. Parents, schools and local businesses are not clamouring to promote the local SACRE. The stakeholder groups most likely to exert public pressure on a SACRE's behalf are religious communities, and this returns us to the difficulty that the work of RE is therefore seen as religious, rather than educational.

SACREs are also responsible for collective worship in community schools,[13] a highly controversial requirement that too often confuses and embarrasses the educational profile of RE. Many parents, school leaders and local authority directors are willing to defend RE but have very different feelings about collective worship; the identification of the two under the umbrella of SACREs exacerbates the problem of isolation, and further weakens the claim to be taken seriously as educators.

The name 'SACRE' is a convenient abbreviation for a long title. Aurally the name is suggestive of sacredness, difference, specialness: it reinforces the religious much more than the educational. This may seem a superficial point, but when combined with the reality that few local authorities understand how to use their SACREs and none have any equivalent bodies for other curriculum subjects, the result is to give symbolic strength to RE's difference, underscoring a sense of its separateness from the wider curriculum and from local authority policy initiatives. The name isolates and incarcerates RE.

Isolation from the community, and from the wider curriculum, is not good for RE. In 2007, several SACREs took part in nationally-funded training and development for the new secondary curriculum, benefiting from professional development time offered to all national curriculum subjects. They had opportunities to think afresh about the curriculum design of their subject, its relationship to skills, and its potential connections to wider curriculum dimensions. Those that refused the invitation passed up an opportunity to understand how learning and curriculum design could change in RE as it was doing in other subjects.

In another example of isolation, the discourse in some SACREs on spiritual and moral development confuses several different priorities such as transmission of cultural identity, transmission or promotion of values and forms of behaviour, and propagating religious truths against secularism. SACREs, isolated from wider, more rigorous discourses and protected from accountability, have tended to adopt such priorities and project them on to RE. Narratives of moral decline, and the need to 'tell' young people what is right and wrong, have entered local RE discourse without any regard for the science of moral development. Narratives of the religious nature of the subject, the Christian heritage of this country, or the superior truth claims of Christianity have sometimes intervened unchecked in the construction of local agreed syllabuses.

A solution to this self-incarceration is offered by Robin Alexander's Cambridge Review of primary education. Alexander recommended community curriculum panels for each local authority, with a non-statutory remit to help implement the whole curriculum. He imagined that the panels would do this by identifying local needs and opportunities, leaving schools with autonomy over how the whole curriculum and its subjects are named, timetabled and taught.[14] This proposal was not framed specifically with RE in mind, but it would, if ever implemented, provide an elegant contribution to resolving our subject's structural weaknesses.

Public evaluation of SACRE effectiveness has been limited by the impulse to control expenditure and avoid seeming to undermine local determination. Until 2010–11, SACREs were regularly sending their own annual reports to the curriculum agency at national level. This body, most recently named the Qualifications and Curriculum Development Agency, received the reports but was not mandated to do anything with them. This body has now been abolished without any accompanying change in the legal requirement on SACREs to send their report to it. SACREs are thus in a position of being obliged to report to a vacuum, and this increases their own sense of isolation, and the appearance of futility.

Such evaluation as there has been, however, paints a picture of SACREs as small, dedicated local bodies, battling against local authority apathy, proud of their local achievements for RE and hyper-vigilant against the incursions of central government. The national association of SACREs has encouraged self-evaluation and has developed tools for use by those SACREs that wish to undertake it. Even the composing of the most recent self-evaluation toolkit, a modest and supportive document designed to enable SACREs to be self-critical and to plan for their improvement, was greeted with suspicion by some SACREs which felt implicitly criticized by the assumption that they could improve. Many SACREs have tended to resist any form of accountability to the centre, preferring to be accountable locally to bodies that do not understand how to use them. This has seldom worked well, and has squandered some opportunities for collaboration, for example at regional and national levels.

Global and local determination

The main argument so far in this chapter has been that SACRE structures are unfair and ineffective, creating a downward pressure on coherence and standards of RE in schools. However, two major factors, affecting several national education systems, must be taken into account. The first is globalization and the access to information technology. Access to information and reflection about religions and philosophies is now rich and instantaneous in nearly all schools. At the touch of a button, I can learn, or teach, about different beliefs, practices, experiences and values; I can watch vivid footage of rituals that give insights to beliefs, or news stories that raise ethical issues.

In this new context, to what extent am I helped by an expectation of compliance with a local authority document? To be sure, the local distribution of religions, and the particular denominational or national form they take, is relevant, but not the only reference point. If my local Muslim community is predominantly Sunni, I shall still want to learn and teach about both Sunni and Shia forms, and do so in a critical and nuanced way. If my local Hindu community practises caste distinctions, I shall still want to encounter those other Hindu believers who reject caste as immoral and alien to Dharma. By the same logic, elements such as the history of the bible, the critical approach to studying the life of Jesus, or the conduct of arguments for and against God's existence, are objects of global scholarship that can be made available in any classroom by a skilled teacher, regardless of municipal boundaries. The notion that the major enquiries of RE change from one local authority community to another, or that the nature of progress in understanding religion or belief changes from one borough to another, is outdated, if it ever had any substance to begin with.

The second major factor is the introduction of the localism agenda, which has given an extra dimension to the case against SACREs as presently composed. The introduction of a diverse number of types of school, each with its own legal or contractual relationship to local or national government, and its own different curriculum obligations, has impacted on RE. According to the 2010 Guidance,[15] there are eight different types of school, each with differing RE requirements, and this predates the arrival of free schools. The localism legislation of the coalition government has considerably heightened the expectation that local communities and individuals will have unprecedented rights and freedoms.[16] In this new context, SACREs are an inadequate vehicle, not because they are local but because they are not local enough. The conditions that influence what should be taught in RE are mostly global and national; but the availability of religious and other communities, as resources, is community, not county based; the variances in quality of RE are between schools, not between counties; and the variances in progress in RE are within-school. SACREs are not local enough to address any of these issues with any hope of improvement. An increasingly devolved and minimal national curriculum has become more local and more accessible than most agreed syllabuses, and this trend is likely to continue.

Thus SACREs and agreed syllabuses are neither global nor local; they might be described as semi-local, and they are inhibited from responding effectively to either the global or the local agendas.

Philosophically, local determination of RE, as presently structured, has few arguments in its favour, and few friends other than some SACRE members, advisers and consultants. The strongest argument in favour of current arrangements is that RE is protected from any putative Secretary of State, or national curriculum review, that might shape the subject inappropriately. For example, the argument goes, an atheist Secretary of State might fail to see the educational rationale of RE and legislate to abolish it; or a fundamentalist Christian might try to turn it into an evangelical vehicle. Either of these would be an inappropriate use of national power. The relative obscurity of local determination protects RE from these dangers, while also encouraging creativity and innovation. The disadvantages and weaknesses of the SACRE system are a lesser evil than the risks of national curriculum status.

Even this argument, however, fails to take account of reality, for three reasons. First, RE already is vulnerable to national factors, and its cherished local status has not protected it. School diversification, local authority cuts, the imposition of the English Baccalaureate and the sharp downturn in teacher training numbers have combined to form very severe threats for RE from 2010 onwards.[17] These threats did not originate from a policy of hostility to

RE, but from a neglect of the consequences for it. National neglect of RE has been a far greater problem for the subject, over the decades since 1944, than any imagined national interference. At the time of writing it appears that politicians and civil servants are set to continue the policy of neglect, even when they realize that the law is being flouted in relation to the duties of local authorities and entitlements of children.

Second, inappropriate intervention can and does happen at local level. In 2006, one local authority found its newly agreed syllabus legally challenged at the final moment by a Christian group on the council, claiming that there was not enough Christianity in the syllabus. Those who argue that local determination has insulated RE from inappropriate interference, and protected the pupils from indoctrination, are right only up to a point: they have forgotten that the unaccountable power interests of religious groups can operate just as easily at local levels as at national ones, and perhaps more so.

Third, any attempt by a putative Secretary of State to abolish RE, or change its fundamental educational character, would be so egregious as to be checked by underlying legal measures in treaties, and human rights and equality law. Advocates of local determination have tended to amplify the dangers of national curriculum status, while denying indignantly that SACREs have any weaknesses other than under-funding.

If a semi-local system is working badly, should we leave it alone in the name of freedom? Can the RE community be content with a set of arrangements – one can hardly call it a system any more – so compromised by untidiness, exclusivity and a tendency to confusion? The inspection agency has twice signalled publicly a need for government to review the legislative underpinning of RE structures;[18] time will tell, however, whether the structures live long enough to see any review.

The decline of RE's structures

The SACRE and agreed syllabus structures are collapsing. Collateral damage from the actions of the coalition government has caused a combination of factors that weaken the SACRE structures seriously and, in the medium term, fatally. The government's drive towards creating more academies and free schools is intended eventually to create a new system of independent schools detached from local authority control and support. While some SACREs have succeeded in forging new and productive relationships with the new academies in their area, they have no constitutional duty to do so, and no right to expect an academy to respond. The very notion of statutoriness being a protection for RE has been weak currency since 2006 and is now almost worthless in a time of deregulation. Internal surveys in the RE professional community – particularly the survey carried out by the RE teachers' professional association in 2011[19] – reveal increasing levels of non-compliance in schools with regard to the legal requirement to teach RE, particularly to 14–16-year-old pupils.

We can infer from the survey that schools are operating within a broadly deregulated environment in which they are aware of being non-compliant but feel that the risk of being found out or forced to change is minimal. Many schools have also responded to the government's inducements to prioritize student options in history and geography in examinations at 16, but not religious studies – the so-called English Baccalaureate – by reducing their RE departments to a minimum. The same survey predicted that more schools would do this in 2012–13.

Wider factors have also weakened RE's current structures. The redundancies of local advisers and reduction in consultants, who have been so crucial in leading SACREs, are creating a vacuum in local RE, which will, in time, make it more possible for a diversity of RE models to spring up. Some of these will be influenced by creative curriculum design and pedagogy, while others will be egregious and educationally inappropriate. There will be very limited capacity in the system to propagate the former or challenge the latter. The severe downturn in funded places for initial teacher training, hitting several subjects but particularly RE, places in jeopardy the future supply of qualified, competent teachers of the subject.

A major factor affecting the future structures of RE is the probable shape of the current curriculum review. While the review focuses solely on the national curriculum, and does not therefore include RE, its direction will create a curriculum and schooling climate in which RE must exist. In particular, the way in which the wider curriculum is structured will be so influential on curriculum design and pedagogy in schools that RE will inevitably be influenced. The review has already signalled an intention to simplify the design of curriculum documents, with narrative descriptions of that which is to be learned matching clear, precise outcomes specific to key stages.[20] It has also reported a concern with the inflexibility and opaqueness of generic eight-level scales and attainment targets across all subjects, and hints at an intention to replace them with a 'simpler system that is also more valid'.[21] The reviewers are interested in a curriculum that prioritizes depth and authentic learning, focusing on fewer things in greater depth at primary phase, and using conceptual understanding and a mastery model in both primary and secondary phases.[22] Here we see some proposals that could indirectly help RE to address its own structural weaknesses: content-led syllabus design, content-heavy teaching, incoherent links between content and assessment, confusion about attainment targets, breadth of coverage trumping depth and integrity of understanding. It is possible to envisage an emerging, non-statutory RE document, a successor to the national framework of 2004, that will mirror the structure of other subjects' programmes of study, and help shape the design of RE so that it overcomes its structural weaknesses. This path is not without difficulty, but the prize – a more coherent design for RE, with or without surviving local structures – is considerable.

Naturally enough, many in the RE community are fighting for the survival of the present structures. Meanwhile, however, there is a need for others to consider what will come after them, and to seize the opportunity to address RE's historically inherited weaknesses.

Conclusion

As a system unique to RE, local determination effectively announces that RE is completely different, works to a different rationale and pedagogical rules from any other subject, and is not required to explain itself in the terms of the rest of the curriculum. If local custodians of RE do not wish to talk the discourse of the wider curriculum, they cannot be required to. They can take RE offshore.

Offshore RE can thrive unchecked in several SACREs and agreed-syllabus conferences because of the group and committee structure and lack of accountability. Where it thrives, it influences teaching and learning processes. The moral deficit of SACRE structures and processes is too often transferred to curriculum design and pedagogy, exposing RE to moral hazard. The SACRE structure absolves those who do not wish to think educationally or play by educational rules. They do not even have to enter into arguments about education: they can simply cry 'local determination'. They can justify RE in parochial or religious terms more than educational ones. This makes for conventional, didactic and weak teaching, and sometimes teaching that inappropriately attempts to advocate a religious outlook on life.

The local determination system creates the possibility of excellence and innovation but also permits unaccountability, confusion, mediocrity or egregious models of the subject – models which treat pupils and classrooms as laboratories for ideas. It is an ironic and unwelcome reality that, after decades in which some SACRE leaders have suspected central government of a plot to kill off local determination, it is now dying, not by agency but by neglect. Its demise creates an opportunity for new structures that appropriately support a model of RE with educational and democratic integrity. The next chapter argues that such a model requires each teacher to have a deeper focus on the significance of pedagogy.

Response from Clive Erricker

What Mark has raised is a deep problem of the disfunctionality of structures and policies. By being effectively unaccountable to and divorced from their constituency in education – schools and learners – religious representatives on SACREs can operate a policy that is self-serving, with a surprising amount of educational ignorance. This leads to a disposition that regards their 'home' constituency, their faith community, as the only really important agency that they represent. In turn, this can mean that religious SACRE representatives see their role not only as ensuring their faith community is faithfully represented (in their terms) but that religion generally is positively approved of in the way it is taught in schools. What a wonderful opportunity to exercise some reverse discrimination against secularism.

Even in a relatively effective SACRE the problems can still remain. When one new agreed syllabus was ready to be implemented a meeting was arranged of the three joint SACREs who were to endorse it for their local constituencies. At this meeting a voluble Christian minority argued against its inclusion of humanism, which then had to be erased from the main body of the text. The complete removal of any mention of humanism from the syllabus was only prevented by the educational representatives on the SACRE actually booing the Christian dissenters when they demanded further deletions to erase humanism entirely. When we speak of offshore agencies SACREs are quite a good example.

Part 3

The case for a radical transformation of RE

Chapter 7

The doors of pedagogical perception

Pedagogy as existential stance

Clive Erricker and Mark Chater

Opening story

They both knew it was going to be a difficult meeting. The coordinator of Key Stage 1 (for pupils aged 5 to 7) was not looking forward to telling her experienced colleague, the teacher in charge of Year 2, that there was a problem with the way she taught RE. The teacher of Year 2 was unhappy for personal reasons and mortified at the prospect of having to discuss her classroom failure with the coordinator.

It had come to this because of a parental complaint. Following the local syllabus, the teacher had attempted to give a lesson on different names for God, using teachings and stories from Christianity and Islam. The material suggested by the syllabus included phrases describing God as a 'loving, forgiving father' (Christianity) and as 'the Lord of all the worlds' (Islam). On the surface it was a good lesson: there was discussion of what these phrases meant, the pupils were happily engaged in role play and there was the beginning of a good display with pictures of forgiving fathers and a great king amongst several planets. The teacher did not find it easy to teach RE, and particularly this lesson, because she had recently lost her own personal faith in God. In teaching the material, she felt hypocritical, awkward and over-exposed. She felt that, if there was a God, he would probably not forgive her; she did not understand what 'Lord of all the worlds' meant, and dreaded someone asking.

At 3p.m., a parent called in and began a conversation with her child and the teacher. The boy showed his picture of 'Lord of all the worlds' and the parent asked what it meant. The boy said it was God but he did not know why. The teacher, very embarrassed, had to admit she did not know either, but it was in the syllabus and she had to teach it. This was overheard by two passing Muslim parents, who were perturbed about drawing pictures of God, and offered to come in and talk to the class about their beliefs. The boy's mother was appalled by this idea, and went straight to the head teacher with a threat to withdraw her son, her reason being that: 'If them lot are allowed in, well, I'm sorry, but will any of our kids be safe?'

In this way it came to the attention of the coordinator that an apparently well-conducted lesson had in reality made little progress in understanding symbolic words and phrases to describe an aspect of religion. On top of this, an experienced and competent teacher was accidentally caught in a geopolitical misunderstanding, and was close to tears with an overwhelming sense of inadequacy and confusion about her role. 'It's not fair to blame me', she said. 'I'm delivering the syllabus. It's just that I don't understand what it's about and why people get so het up. Anyway I don't agree with foisting God on them when they're that young; look at the damage it does in the world.'

Introduction

This chapter introduces the idea that pedagogy derives first and foremost from existential stance: the way in which we conceive of our role in relation to the overall development of young people whom we are responsible for educating. This is elaborated upon by presenting a chain of pedagogical development to show how a competent teacher takes into account the linked pedagogical factors that influence the immediate time and place of learning. The chapter then turns to an analysis of how RE is impoverished if the links in the pedagogical chain are weak.

Pedagogy and existential stance

In Chapter 3 we established that pedagogy must mean more than the methods chosen by the teacher in planning and implementing RE. The case was made that pedagogy in RE requires a coherent understanding of the human condition, society, the paradigm of knowledge implicit in the discipline and subject matter, and the ways in which learners, in their context, will apprehend the ideas on offer. The understanding of these variant factors, and how they influence learning, should be seen as a set rather than a random collection. Teachers must work at understanding these factors for themselves as part of pedagogical preparation. Pedagogy is a personal existential stance before it is anything else.

In the introduction to their edited work *If Classrooms Matter*, Jeffrey Di Leo and Walter Jacobs outline their idea of what it means to speak of a classroom.[1] It is determined by 'place, pedagogy and politics'.[2] Moreover, sites of pedagogy should be understood as 'places of interaction and struggle'.[3] It follows, they argue, that a pedagogical space 'should be regarded as local and contingent (non-generalizable and non-universalizable)'.[4] At a simple level, teachers should be able to recognize such features in their everyday practice; for example a lesson that works with one class seems to fail with another – and yet it was the same lesson. What was different was the interaction that took place, which was dependent on a number of variable factors: the type of class, the composition of individuals within it, the mode of delivery (for example the technology used); the time of day or day of the week; events that had happened prior to the class, for teacher and students, affecting their states of mind.

Di Leo and Jacobs want to extend these variables and the nature of what we understand as sites of pedagogy and the 'classroom' further than the everyday and the traditional school. They refer to how:

> The contemporary reconfiguration of the classroom can be broken down into three interrelated modes or dimensions. The first mode concerns physical transformations of the classroom, that is to say, reconfigurations of the place or space of teaching and learning. The second mode concerns pedagogical transformations, or reconfigurations of the relations between the place of learning and the human participants engaged in learning and teaching. The third mode concerns institutional or political transformations at work regarding the classroom, that is to say, the cultural and political aspects.[5]

The first dimension obviously includes classroom layouts. Choices about the configuration of desks and chairs, such as rows of desks facing the front or groups of desks that advertise more collaboration and discussion, are significant indicators of classroom architecture for particular pedagogical modes. However, the point being made is that 'classroom' can be understood in a far wider way, consistent with where learning can take place. Pedagogic sites can be other than within the traditional school site, and certainly young people learn and are subject to enculturation in various places that they visit in their everyday lives, both physical and virtual. The idea of school trips is an indication of this and, for RE teachers, visits to places of worship, holocaust sites and museums etc. are a regular feature in many schools. But, also, students are influenced in both attitude and inclinations by their 'out of school' experiences of sites that are a regular feature of their life or a lack of variety in such experiences. For example, Clive was present at a conference day for RE GCSE students, where students went to a variety of workshops. Individual students in turn had to answer questions from the others. One female student was asked what activities she did in her free time with her friends. Her answer was she went shopping. When asked what else she did, she answered 'nothing'. If one imagined the possibility of a conversation she might have with someone from a society in which there were no shopping malls, nor a culture of consumerism, one starts to get a sense of the limitations and difficulties of cross-cultural understanding and its relevance that might be in place when trying to broaden and deepen such a student's development.

The second dimension, reconfigurations of the relations between the place of learning and the human participants engaged, is directly related to the idea of locality and contingency mentioned above. In a simple way we can apply this by saying that we know that the quality of relationship between learners and teachers affects classroom behaviour, the quality of the learning environment and progress in learning. Some teachers are aware that this is a significant factor in promoting success in their classes, and make this a high priority; others do not, and fall back on rules and threats because of this deficiency. But this quality can change with a new class, a new school and different cohorts of students: thus an example of both locality and contingency. On a different level individuality is at work, because it is a crude categorization just to say a classroom or pedagogical site is made up of a teacher and the learners. It is better to think in a more sophisticated way of the opportunities for learning available and the best way in which they can be promoted: who can learn from whom, what interactions and organization can facilitate that; also, bearing in mind that there is an existential quality to learning, making important the confidence of students to draw on their own experience in a relevant way and enrich the learning of others by voicing it. For a simple example Clive can draw on his experience of observing a lesson in a school near Farnborough, where Nepalese students were part of the class and just beginning to learn to use English as their means of expression (they were there because a Gurkha regiment was stationed nearby). At the beginning of the class they were rather lost and clearly occupied the role of pupils with learning difficulties. But, as the lesson went on they were drawn in by being asked to speak of their own experiences of being in England and Nepal, the reasons why they were there and difficulties they had encountered. Not only did this raise their confidence and participation, but others were learning from them and starting to see them in a new light.

The third dimension, the cultural and political aspects of the classroom, or the politics of pedagogical space, necessitates dialogue with general aspects of culture and society. In other words there are political and cultural contexts which determine why we understand the classroom and pedagogy in the ways that we do, and how those contexts impinge on our very idea of education and where and how it takes place. The struggles over this dimension are evident in the political and cultural history of the UK; as examples affecting RE, we could cite the move to comprehensive, all-ability secondary schools, the shifts in rationale and approach to RE and the influence of a succession of strategies for dealing with diversity, such as multiculturalism and community cohesion. Religious education, in particular, is a highly political (as well as cultural) subject because of the strong doctrinal, prejudicial and moral messages propounded by some religious bodies over such issues as birth control, abortion and homosexuality. It is partly because of this that some teachers decline to address these issues as a matter for enquiry and debate and instead teach the subject 'factually' and with caution. The subject has, as a result, been criticized for its delivery of too much 'learning about' and not enough 'learning from', in the parlance of the attainment targets presently in place in most syllabuses. This is an example of the way in which teachers of religious education may consciously seek to avoid the political dimension of pedagogy, and treat the cultural dimension blandly as a matter of factual input. The effect of this negligence in approach was brought home to Clive at another conference for GCSE students, where a panel of religious experts from different faiths was set up to answer students' questions. One question the panel was asked to respond to was in relation to religions' antipathy to homosexuality. In turn each panel member answered that homosexuality was wrong, even abhorrent, giving differing reasons. One panel member even suggested that homosexuals needed to be sent to psychiatrists. Then, a Jewish member of the panel pointed out that he was homosexual and stayed in his religious community to try to change these opinions. What was striking was that the panel members, up to that point, had assumed there were no homosexuals present – such was their arrogance and sense of self-righteousness. Homosexuals were clearly the non-present 'others'. Clearly, this was an indication that RE should be addressing this issue in order, at the least, to make the subject relevant to students' concerns and to foster a proper democratic debate in the classroom that is politically prescient. It is also an indication that religions were not interested in endorsing, let alone celebrating, forms of diversity to which they were opposed.

It is difficult to see how anyone involved in education could legitimately counter the argument that students need to be aware of how societies are run. They also need to know what the various influences at work in them are, how these affect particular groups and the issues of representation and acceptance that arise as a result, and how that connects to larger issues relating to globalization. If it is not the case that young people are properly accustomed to, and politically literate within, democratic societies then what exactly is democratically wrong with the societies in question? Education has the task of ensuring this happens and that schools, classrooms and other educating initiatives are the significant sites for this. This is why we must understand pedagogy at this deeper level and 'classrooms' as more than rooms in which subjects are taught. In this context the study of religion and its role in national and global affairs is crucial because of its pervasive influence. At the same time religion cannot be studied in isolation but as an integrated aspect of why the world is as it is, how it might change or be changed, and forms of agency that different groups occupy in trying to achieve different ends. The 'sites' of learning in RE therefore include any places where religion or belief is considered in the public sphere: the House of Lords, the local council, hospitals, cemeteries, cinemas, and the print and networked media. These sites must be visited, physically and culturally, as part of RE: they form part of the (often unacknowledged) existential stance of both learner and teacher.

In a time of various sorts of protest against different types of authority with vested interests – at the time of writing, the Arab spring, the Occupy movements, the financial slump and controversy over corporate greed, and the paedophile issue within the Roman Catholic Church – all have significance in determining how we understand our society and our world. It is for educationalists to introduce young people to these issues, at an appropriate time, as a preparation for their democratic responsibilities and their rights and social responsibilities. Ignorance of these matters would amount to educational failure. This is where our pedagogical thinking should be centred on the political affairs of what it means to be a citizen.

Henry Giroux writes:

> With few exceptions the project of democratizing public goods has fallen into disrepute in the popular imagination as the logic of the market undermines the most basic social solidarities. The consequences include not only a weakened state but a growing sense of insecurity, cynicism and political retreat on the part of the general public.[6]

Whether one agrees with this statement at the level of fact, or disputes its importance in terms of values, it is highly important to understand such commentary on public affairs and weigh its value. Countless other statements encompassing differing stances could also be produced. What is important is that students should be educated in such a way that they develop towards being able to comment and take part in debate on issues such as these, central to the quality of their lives. If that is our aim then the pedagogue's first task is to work out how we help young people achieve that development, rather than end up as part of the tabloid readership or just ignoring the news as irrelevant.

Analysing the approaches of Di Leo, Jacobs and Giroux it is clear that their first priority is the development of young people into becoming active, informed democratic citizens with critical awareness, a project which can be achieved by putting at their disposal the widest range of opportunities possible in their education.

In one school Clive has worked with, they took this understanding of developing young people for active and confident participation in the world very seriously and made it the basis of all that took place in the curriculum: everything had to attend to that aim. The head teacher stated this in terms of developing young people in order for them to be able to live in an autonomous and authentic way. These were unusual terms to bring to a staff of teachers, let alone classroom assistants, catering staff and others. But the point was this: students in the school lived on a large housing estate, previously the largest in Europe, and rarely ventured off it. When the school made job placements available for work experience, very few opted for those off the estate and the ones on it were oversubscribed. This was evidence of their lack of confidence in engaging beyond their normal environment and the limitation of their horizons. The school aim to contribute to their living autonomous and authentic lives (by the time they were 25-year-old adults) was intended to ensure they maximized their life opportunities in both an economic and a socio-cultural sense. But the school also addressed the idea of them needing to recognize that they were responsible for their own futures and needed to be morally responsible for their life-stances at the same time.

In effect, the head teacher's vision was existential, not just focused on prescriptive educational demands regarding attainment, though it also encompassed these. During Clive's time in supporting this project he was aware how the school also engaged with parents and leaders of the local community to try and make this possible. Also, it developed a values education programme, based on the methodology of the Hampshire Agreed Syllabus for Religious Education, which was at the centre of this development. The values programme covered religious education, citizenship and personal, social and health education (PSHE) in an integrated fashion.[7] Religious education was not lost or distorted in this venture, rather it became a central hub in its implementation, and had palpable pedagogical impact precisely because it was an intentional element in a larger vision that included sites and factors beyond the school.

The project that the head teacher has embarked upon goes beyond the usual mantras of current educational rhetoric such as 'learning for life' or lifelong learning or the emphasis on knowledge and skills. Such sound bites mask the problems of education by reducing them to particulars affecting the state of our economy and its competitiveness. This is not to say, for example, that continuing a lifelong habit of learning is not beneficial or that knowledge and skills are not also. But the context in which they are 'delivered' is one of the accumulation of capital owned by those who control the education system, not by those who work directly with young people. In that sense, such phrases are capitalist propaganda. By contrast, the existential quality of the head teacher's vision discussed above is more deep-rooted and fundamentally attuned to students' needs as democratic citizens, not just labourers in the economic market, even though knowledge, skills and the desire to continue learning will be outcomes of it. The notions of autonomy and authenticity are radically opposed to just getting what you need to get to serve the system. They encourage thought and conviction as well: they are political in the best sense of that term. In contrast, Chris Falk, as Erica McWilliam observes, regards lifelong learning as 'sentencing learners to life'; it works as a vehicle for selling commodities and as a profitable commodity in itself. To Falk, lifelong learning 'is largely a project of economic, social and epistemological recuperation dedicated to delimiting rather than expanding the subjectivities of learners exposed to it'.[8]

In the Autumn of 2011 we both, independently of each other, went to visit the Occupy London movement outside St Paul's Cathedral. We only discovered this fact many months later, in the writing of this chapter. Clive had been interested in whether it was an effective protest or not, and he met with one of the working groups it had set up. This consisted of four young people, early twenties to mid-thirties, who were working on a protest aimed at the imminent G20 summit. They were enthusiastic and, most importantly, realized, as they described it, that they were contributing to constructing a democratic process within the camp in order to make constructive demands that all those there would agree to. Mark had been curious about the implied spirituality and values of the various posters and flags – 'nature is the only superpower', 'we are the 99 per cent' – and had conversations with people in the spirituality tent and the learning tent, the latter a self-styled university where all ideas were on offer from members of the camp teaching each other. We both felt that, whatever else it was, this was a learning experience they would remember all their lives. In the evening there was an assembly when all working groups reported and those present voted for particular recommendations. Eventually this lead to a series of points being set out as what the protest demanded in terms of change. It was eminently practical and precise, and provided an effective model of how democratic learning towards decision making could take place in schools. Everything that occurred in the process that the protesters had set up could simply be transferred into the upper primary and secondary school contexts. The eagerness of those in the working groups, their desire to work for the common good, their recognition that they were working with others for a consensus, and the responsibility they felt to arrive at specific outcomes, was all so characteristic of a democratic education handling values with purpose and fearlessness. This, of course, is the opposite of what corporate finance is about, and the antithesis of practice in many schools. The Occupy London movement actually shames us educators.

What the Occupy London movement exemplifies chimes with the ethical dimension to the aims and purposes set out in the Cambridge Review of primary education. One passage in the review says this:

> There needs to be a new set of aims that drive the curriculum, teaching, assessment, schools and policy. The aims and purposes proposed by the Review unashamedly reflect values and moral purposes, for that is what education is about. They are designed to empower children to manage life and find meaning in the twenty-first century. They reflect a coherent view of what it takes to become an educated person.
>
> These aims are inter-dependent. For instance, empowerment and autonomy are achieved in part through exploring, knowing, understanding and making sense, through the development of skill and freeing of imagination, and through the power of dialogue. Should such a set of aims be statutory? The Review leaves this question open for debate.[9]

In stressing the inter-dependence of elements such as empowerment and knowledge, the review points up the politics of epistemology. If RE wishes to take account of this inter-dependence, it will find effective responses in paying attention to the power relations that influence every site of learning, every individual teacher and learner.

The chain of pedagogical development

In accordance with the view that learning works best when it pays attention to its situatedness in political contexts, we can speak of the necessity for building a chain of pedagogical development. This is envisaged as a chain because it links the largest global economic and cultural forces, through a series of connections, to the most specific sites of learning in classrooms and other places. It begins with the underlying economic and socio-cultural contextual realities imbibed by student and teacher alike; moves on through existential stance until we get to classroom activity via the possibility of methodology. A competent teacher of RE moves up and down this chain with facility, and enables learners to do the same. Where the chain is weak or broken or even little understood in RE (perhaps an example of RE's isolationism), this makes for pedagogy that lacks coherence or integrity. Other subjects also require a similar chain, though it is differently linked in each subject. For RE, the sequence of links consists of:

- *Global and national context*: economic, cultural and moral forces: discourses on our nation's learning are increasingly influenced by economics and a need to remain competitive with regard to skills and knowledge. The application and misapplication of international measures such as PISA (the OECD Programme for International Student Assessment) are one feature of the discourse. It is permitted to shape the breadth of the curriculum and overshadow discussions of the worth of qualifications. The cultural context of how the nation understands itself and its heritage is a parallel discourse, operating frequently by pulling in opposite directions to the economic. For example, economic imperatives are said to be driving the need for mathematics, sciences and modern foreign languages. Cultural imperatives drive a specific set of definitions of methodology and content selection in subjects such as history and English. Moral discourses exist at global levels, for example in relation to ideological conflicts, concerns about children's health and well-being, and discourses on human rights and entitlement. RE has a non-existent narrative for economic purposes and only a tenuous one for cultural. Both of these could be developed if the subject were to evolve. Its moral discourse is strong because RE teachers share a sense of existential stance in relation to the status and survival of the subject itself, and the inherent importance of studying religion and being informed, empathetic, literate or articulate about it. Teachers of RE also need to have reflected on their own personal beliefs, whether religious, philosophical or existential, and their sense of identity in relation to communities of belief. This reflection is essential if a teacher is to be relaxed about handling beliefs critically.

- *National definitions of education and curriculum*: at legislative level, the economic and cultural context, as understood and interpreted by policy makers, passes down into definitions of the aims and purposes of the school curriculum. This also includes a range of subjects that look increasingly arbitrary and largely unchanged from the late nineteenth century.

- *Definitions of rationale and scope for subjects* (e.g. importance statements or equivalents): for RE, the chain frequently breaks or has a weak link at this point. Often, interpretations of context and definitions of overall curriculum aims fail to find their way into subjects, because subjects are defined by content and content remains inert. This is accentuated in RE because local syllabuses do not all use the same importance statement, and this leads to considerable blurring of the purposes of the subject in the context of the wider curriculum. There is also a failure to make reference to the overall aims of the curriculum and how they can be enacted in RE. This type of weakness arises from RE's historical isolation as a locally determined subject.

- *Definitions of progress in subjects* (e.g. attainment targets and level statements): although RE has a wide consensus on learning about and learning from, this model is in need of clarification, as discussed in Chapter 3. It particularly needs a more resilient link to the rationale and aims. This is the second weak link.

- *Subject signature pedagogies*: examples of these distinctive, discipline-influenced pedagogies exist in other subjects, such as citizenship, where a distinctive feature of learning is the idea of making change happen through activism, and in science, which employs a particular form of enquiry. RE has no agreed signature pedagogy, and most agreed syllabuses, with one exception,[10] have backed away from defining pedagogy, though all have an implicit or default pedagogy (the coverage of religions). This is the third weak link.

- *Teachers' apprehensions of all the above*: their capacity to be self-critical about sense of purpose and take a critical perspective not only in relation to their own practice but the whole chain of pedagogic design and their mediation of it.

- *The construction of a teaching and learning methodology*: an essential component of becoming a teacher, e.g. through exposure to gifted mentor teachers, ongoing professional development, and academic study of teaching and learning methodologies, and their provenance, in university courses that are now being allowed or forced to close.

- *Teachers' choice of classroom strategies/activities and techniques*: only this last point is above the surface, and even then to varying degrees; the rest of the pedagogic iceberg lies beneath it. Schools are often only addressing what appears above the surface, especially in relation to the statistics concerning attainment and progress. Thus we finally exhaust the capacity for teachers to improve attainment and progress by only addressing technique, and at the same time we exhaust the teachers and the statistics level off.

Taking the chain as a whole, RE is of mixed strength in the first link because, while it has a strong sense of its own moral and spiritual importance, it has little to say on economic factors and an ambiguous claim to relevance on cultural issues. RE's key weak links are in the third, fourth and fifth links in the chain, relating to rationale, attainment and signature pedagogy. In the sixth, seventh and eighth links, relating to ordinary definitions of reflective practice and classroom performance, there is no evidence that RE teachers are inadequate in large numbers, but the proportion of good or outstanding teaching in RE lags behind all other subjects, with the strongest causative factor being a lack of clarity about purpose in teaching.[11] The classroom performance of teachers of RE can be excellent and inspiring, or competent but built on slippery foundations. However, excellent classroom practice, if dependent upon incomplete or blurred understandings of rationale and progress, can still be highly problematic for learners and the subject; a chain is only as strong as its weakest link.

Thus there can be dissonance between an existential stance and its translation into the purposes of learning in itself, and from purposes to actuality. These categories are often confused and seldom securely related – a weakness in the links affecting both student progress and teachers' aims. This can also have a negative impact on the profile and reputation of the subject.

The energy and conviction of outstanding teachers of RE can be conceived as the extent to which they are able to secure all the links in this pedagogical chain, to use all the links as part of the context for learning on a variety of sites, and to understand their own personal vocation and professional competence to teach as a coherent set of answers to the questions posed by each link in the chain. This calls into question older precepts of RE teaching such as 'bracketing out' personal beliefs or assumptions. Not only is the teacher entitled to such beliefs; he or she must work on them, subject them to critical reflection, and find ways to narrate them as part of the shared discourse with learners. Thus it can happen that a discussion on 'why we have to do RE' becomes a discussion on different religious, secular or philosophical ways of seeing the world, and the impact those worldviews have on the world in which that class of young people are learning to take their place. A proper attention to the chain frees learners from fixation with certain 'default' aims of education, and frees teachers and learners from 'default' teaching modes such as didacticism.

The doors of perception: existential stances and curriculum politics

So far the argument has been that a teacher of RE should have regard to the widest possible context in consciously shaping his or her pedagogical stance; that a pedagogical stance, far from being a technical matter of methods to select, is a profound and complex personal existential frame of belief and value. This is not an easy ethic to live by, as the opening story shows: but it is an honest one, and its vindication lies in its ambition to design learning in RE so that it makes a clear contribution to the highest hopes of communities, and so that each individual professional can articulate what he or she is doing and why.

The vision of a chain of pedagogical development, bringing secure understanding and freedom to each individual professional, has many obstacles, and in this section we consider the main problems in terms of curriculum policy and professional culture.

Curriculum policy has generally been of limited help, and sometimes a positive hindrance, to the creation of a chain of pedagogical development. As discussed in Chapter 2, education policy has contained mixed messages with regard to compliance and freedom. Successive iterations of the national curriculum in England have been highly prescriptive and encouraged a content-led, delivery approach in the professional culture of teachers. This state of affairs has acted as an obscuring cloud on the vision of pedagogical development. In recent years, three English-based reviews – the official secondary curriculum of 2007, the semi-official Rose review of the primary curriculum in 2009 and the independent Cambridge Review of primary education in 2010 – have gone some way to encouraging teachers to step through the door into pedagogical freedom and responsibility, but in each case these reviews have had limited traction.

The secondary curriculum of 2007[12] had broadly been re-designed with a central focus on what the system wanted to achieve with young people, academically and socially, very much congruent with the approach outlined earlier of Di Leo, Jacobs and Giroux. The emphasis on learner development was clear, with the three overriding aims of enabling young people to become successful learners, confident individuals and responsible citizens. The diagrammatic presentation of the curriculum – the 'big picture' – placed subjects in such a way that their worth was to be judged on the extent that they contributed to these aims for young people, rather than (as before) merely being knowledge founded solely on intrinsic subject criteria. This innovative curriculum had clear pedagogical implications. Backed by statute and an extensive professional development programme, it gained powerful momentum in secondary schools but was incompletely understood in many of them, particularly in relation to the aims and key concepts. A majority of schools focused on mechanistic forms of delivery through skills, and continued to follow the curriculum mainly in terms of content delivery. An opportunity to widen the open door of pedagogical insight and freedom was wasted in the way teachers and schools thought about their role in confined terms.

The Rose-led review of the primary curriculum, reporting in 2009,[13] essayed a similar vision and was well supported by primary professionals because it reflected the most progressive pedagogies characterized by active, real-world learning. Using the same three aims, it particularized the curriculum in primary context, rather than (as in previous primary curricula) simply organizing content so that it was a primary preparation for secondary content. The Rose model had a central hub of skills, values and attitudes, called 'essentials for learning and life',[14] addressing the whole-person development of the primary-school child. This model, like the secondary curriculum of 2007, had clear pedagogical implications, and would have done much to enable teachers to see and use the full length of the chain of pedagogical development. But the entire project was stillborn: the new coalition government in 2010 refused to implement it, and threw away two years of research and consultation.

Both official reviews had the potential to include RE in the form of a non-statutory national document aligned with the format and aims of the wider curriculum. In this way, the benefits of these reviews, albeit limited, were on offer for professionals in the RE community, in the form of a curriculum structure that encouraged teachers to see and use the full context of pedagogy in line with the vision of Di Leo, Jacobs and Giroux.

The coalition government had no obligation to consider the aims advocated by the independent Cambridge Review,[15] let alone any wish to make them statutory. This review advocated a more radical throwing-open of the doors, accompanied by a discourse on the relationship of curriculum and pedagogy that was more complex than the two official reviews. The radical reach of Alexander's vision was something we noted in our earlier discussion of Occupy London. But this vision also has been sidelined. What followed instead was an apparent deregulation of education, still in process, but with the Secretary of State for education keeping a tight hold on curriculum and pedagogy through the newly introduced English Baccalaureate and through official or unofficial sanctioning of particular teaching approaches.

The shambles of halting, compromised curriculum progress followed by sudden reversal has not been conducive to theorizing a causal link between curriculum and pedagogy for RE, or for any subject. Instead, the irrational politics of the curriculum has permitted the growth and persistence of a number of pedagogical myths prevalent in the professional culture of teachers, including those of RE. Among these myths is the false dichotomy of skills versus content: this is the poverty of pedagogical discourse seen when teachers say 'I've got a skills-based approach to RE' as if that were superior to a content-based approach. This is false because a well-worked-out pedagogy brings together the right skills with appropriate content. Another myth in RE, now on the wane but still present, is the notion of readiness, with its assumption that some concepts or belief systems, such as Buddhism, are too complex or culturally distanced for children at certain ages or stages. This is essentially a determinist cast of mind, and has been questioned by constructivist thinking.[16] In RE the concept of readiness is associated with a pedagogy in which teachers see themselves as the providers of information, and learners as people who must receive it. The information will not change and the learners are allowed no active role in making it theirs: therefore they must wait until they are deemed to be developmentally ready. A third myth is that 'learning about' in RE must precede 'learning from' – that information must always come first, and personal response must follow. This myth casts a very long pedagogical shadow, which blots out many interesting potential approaches to RE, ignores methodological questions and instead imposes an impoverished pedagogical template.

There is a need for the RE community to acknowledge the poverty of its pedagogical debate – in which it is far from alone among the subjects. However, competing pedagogies and localisms have exacerbated this poverty. RE can identify solutions to be found in workable existential stances for teachers and in understanding itself as part of a whole curriculum effort.

Conclusion

What will open the doors of pedagogical perception, allowing RE teachers to see the great scope and force of ideas that informs their pedagogy, and encouraging them to shape it consciously as a professional existential stance? At a time when official discourses are making a crude and reductionist binary distinction between curriculum and pedagogy, it will become more challenging to bring the two together in a coherent theory with integrity. In one English local authority, teachers and advisers have shared the experience of writing and implementing an agreed syllabus[17] that consciously brought curriculum and pedagogy together in a developed teaching methodology. This circumstance created leverage so that many teachers were able to have their own chain of pedagogical development critically examined, and their practice transformed. Even so, some teachers and schools were able to hide from this initiative, continuing with largely unconscious and unaccountable methods rather than fully theorized and actioned methodologies.

Finally, what is the point of a methodology? It is systematically to link together a rationale or purpose statement, a definition of attainment and a set of decisions about content, skills and approaches, in such a way that they form a coherent and defensible whole, serving student development and progression in learning. A methodology should be owned by both teachers and learners as an overall process of learning that can be critically and diagnostically assessed for effectiveness.[18] In effect, a methodology is the instrumental point in the pedagogic chain at which the pedagogic philosophy is translated into practice. For RE, improvement and survival depend in large part on paying urgent attention to this in the mind of every teacher and in the collective minds of religious communities. The latter is addressed in Chapter 8.

Towards an educational economy of religions

Mark Chater and Clive Erricker

Opening story

Ben and Nikky are training to be primary teachers. They have been set a task by their RE tutor: to construct some lessons for Year 4 children (aged 8), based on symbols from two religions, Judaism and Hinduism. Using resources to give them some good ideas for a practical approach, they select some questions and tasks related to the Seder plate in Judaism and the avatar Krishna in Hinduism. Taking one symbol each, they decide to conduct a taped interview with a local representative of the religion, discussing the meaning of the symbol. Their plan is to use this interview with the children in order to bring the symbols, and the communities who use them, very much to life.

Ben's interview goes well, he gets his interviewee relaxed and she begins to chat away about the symbol and what it has meant to her and her family. At one point, when Ben suggests another meaning for the symbol, suggested by one of the pupils, the lady smiles and says 'I have not heard that ... but I am sure you are right. There are many meanings to it. Even at my age we are learning new things all the time!' And she laughs.

When Nikky begins to discuss the other symbol with her interviewee, she uses the same technique, and includes some of the questions the pupils have asked. Her interviewee is very firm about the meanings: 'this means ... that refers to ... No, it has nothing to do with the colour. Get it right!' He does not welcome the ideas and questions of the pupils: 'There is only one correct meaning, I'm telling you. You teach them! If you can't get it right don't teach it at all!' The interview ends with embarrassment.

Introduction

Much has been written about the ways in which religions can influence education, through RE and their presence in schools. Religious organizations and theorists of religion and spiritual development have critiqued education systems for their marginalization of religious realities, for propagating relativism and transcendence blindness, and for constructions of the curriculum and knowledge that fail to give proper credence to the reality of faith[1] or for problematizing it without exerting equal scrutiny on secular outlooks and assumptions.[2] Religious communities have also celebrated their own commitment to education and seen it as a vital expression of their mission.[3]

This chapter invites both religious and educational communities to invert the conversation by asking how religious communities are and can be changed by being in education. It is surely improbable that such deep involvement in running schools, shaping RE and encountering young learners in places of worship has left religious communities unchanged. But very little has been written or said about how being an educator, or in touch with educators, might change faith communities, and in particular how it might challenge and redeem them from their own less democratic and less accountable aspects, discussed in Chapter 1.

Put briefly, the question is: does coming into contact with learning change the way people and communities hold their faith? If so, how does this work, and how can it be made to work more? The different experiences of Ben and Nikky, related above, suggest that some individuals and communities of faith are better able to be open to questioning and learning than others. Why is this so, and what factors can help to make them more open to learning?

The educational economy of religions

We are in a courtroom, witnessing an ethical contest in the recent past.

> The Reverend Jim Grove is a wiry and intense man, his eyes burning and hawklike as he takes the measure of each person entering the ninth-floor federal courtroom in downturn Harrisburg. He is among the first people whom visitors encounter as they arrive to watch the trial billed in the media as the second coming of the Scopes monkey trial. 'Yes', Grove says, 'It's a monkey trial all right. And the evolutionists are the monkeys.' He does not smile when he says this. 'Evolution is the road to atheism,' Grove explains. 'Our children's future is at stake.'[4]

By referring back to the 1925 trial of John Scopes, a teacher in Tennessee, for teaching evolution in the classroom, Grove unwittingly shows us that this dispute is part of a long-running conflict between education and religion, or at any rate specific forms of them. In Lawrence and Lee's semi-fictionalised account of the 1925 trial,[5] the rigid and fearful fundamentalism of the prosecutors is itself placed in the dock, and shown to be ridiculous. The trial takes place in front of an audience composed largely of students, who symbolically are witnesses to the conflict. In front of their young eyes, the religion that most of them respect, and some fear, steps into an educational arena and is vanquished by questions it cannot answer intelligently. The young people's fear turns, by the end, to outright mockery. But the rigidities live on, and are again on the march. Encountering educational and intellectual defeat has not changed the fundamentalist movement: on the contrary, humiliation seems to have made it stronger in its certainties. How can this process be reversed and redeemed, and what part can education play?

Nearly all religious and belief traditions and communities have fundamentalist branches. They may be interpreted as aberrant and embarrassing deviations from an intellectual mainstream, in which case they can be dismissed as untypical; or they may be contextualized as expressions of some aspects of a tradition's primary sources – aspects which are educationally in deficit and needing redemption. Hard-wired into many basic religious teachings are profoundly anti-educational sentiments and when these come out into the educational milieu they have to be accounted for. In the Jubilee teaching in Leviticus 24: 44–46, liberties are extended to all except foreign slaves and their children. Thus a utopic and liberative teaching is disfigured, and the tradition carries, as a deficit, this streak of ethnic violence and disregard for children. And in the Qur'an Sura 2: 3–7, we find an itemizing of those who will be saved on the last day and those who will not. The verses promise bliss for some and violent torment for others, meted out by a beneficent God. There are contradictions here, and no defence of cultural accretion or human failing is possible when the texts in question are held to be holy.

Often we find that religious traditions cannot renew themselves – cannot redeem their ethical and intellectual deficit – without conflict and disputation. Organizational theorist Karl Weick promotes the theory of loose coupling to chart the way in which organizations can manage cognitive dissonance in order to create a loose and flexible relationship between their own internal way of seeing the world and the worldviews of external organizations with which they come into contact.[6] The theory began in educational contexts.[7] It is this process which religious communities and organizations need in order to recreate their internal intellectual and educational economy.

A religion can be drawn towards greater integrity by being asked questions, by permitting attention to be drawn to its defects and hypocrisies, and by listening to itself in dialogue with others as it clarifies or improves its position. The questioning needs to be rigorous. Being exposed to the questioning and fearless gaze of the young is a strong democratizing and clarifying discipline for any religion or belief. Pedagogy in RE needs to pay attention to each belief system's degree of willingness to be treated in this way.

The degree of willingness may be likened to a national economy's relative strength. Theologians in the Christian tradition apply the term 'economy' to the Holy Trinity. They try to describe the Trinity as it impacts upon humanity, for example in creation, history, the formation of the church, worship and the everyday life of the believer. Western theologians contrast the economic

Trinity with the immanent Trinity, which describes how and what the Trinity is in itself, its essence or ontology. If the immanent Trinity is how God appears to God, the economy of the Trinity is how God appears to us. In the late modern era, Western theologians have described the Trinity as God's way of being open to the world, eternal and unchanging yet active in temporal contexts.[8] Despite this distinctive open characteristic, the economic Trinity is still fundamentally the same as the immanent Trinity. To encounter the triune God's economy is to encounter God's very self.[9] Economy in this theological sense means the way an idea cashes itself out to people, how the transaction creates change and yet the idea remains essentially the same.

In coining the term 'educational economy', I mean the way in which a religion or belief system behaves educationally and how that behaviour affects its essence. How a religion is in itself, and how it presents itself to questioning and change, may be distinctive and yet ought to be fundamentally the same. Educational economy could be described as a belief system's degree of availability to educational enquiry about itself, its posture in relation to intellectual endeavour, its historical and present commitment to critical thought and questioning. The extent to which a belief system has a strong educational economy is the extent to which it makes itself available to critical enquiry, takes intellectual endeavour seriously in its own right, and commits itself to critical thought. Clearly, some belief systems have stronger educational economies than others. Also, each tradition is diverse in this regard: each has its scholars, each its book-burners; each has its eras of prodigious scholarly energy and intellectual daring, each its periods of introversion and dry dogmatism. The strength of educational economy in one tradition can also vary from continent to continent and town to town, depending on leadership. Nevertheless, any religion or belief in a particular time and place may be said to be more or less open to educational enquiry, and thus have a stronger or weaker educational economy.

This strength, or lack of it, can be measured by various indicators. Some criteria might be: versatility and integrity in interpreting texts; ability to have a rationale for change over time; the manner in which truth claims are held and promulgated; positioning on the exclusivist–inclusivist spectrum; treatment of women and ethnic, sexual and class minorities; relaxation with diversity; acknowledgement of repressive and violent impulses. The shift from transmissive facts and one-dimensional meanings to interactive exchange of ideas is a crucial evolutionary step for belief communities, indicating confidence in their cultural survival and the durability of their teachings.

These factors are indicators of the educational economy of a belief system because they represent a belief system's way of cashing itself out to young enquirers. The indicators themselves may be said to be partial, in the sense that they are representative of a Western enlightenment and modernist cast of mind: other cultures might want other indicators, but these sit closest to the heart of the Western educational project.

That same Western educational project has historically puzzled over these indicators. The antecedents to a concept of educational economy lie in the Western Christian tradition of catechesis. With exceptions, the catechetical discipline has felt ambivalent towards education. Its pedagogical and andragogical thinkers, from Augustine to the present,[10] have tended to make only selective use of educational methods, held back from whole-heartedly embracing education and advocated the use of educational methods only to a certain point and in service of specific pre-determined truths. The most noteworthy and influential exception is the strand of educational thinking and activity originating from Christiane Brusselmans[11] and her colleagues, which developed into the Rite of Christian Initiation of Adults (RCIA). The outcome of a collaboration between catechists of the Roman Catholic Church and developmentalists, the RCIA applied developmental insights to theological education, and influenced the development of textbooks and methods for children and young people also. The RCIA was premised on the idea of the local and universal church as a learning community, changed for the better by its openness to questioning by its own catechands and neophytes. The RCIA's influence is now on the wane, having been replaced by more doctrinally driven models. In the liberal Protestant milieux of the nineteenth and twentieth centuries, which saw education and models of RE gradually distancing themselves from the power of the church and the absolutes of revelation, the relationship with pedagogical processes has predominantly been one of uneasy negotiation[12] rather than educational commitment.

If the educational economy of a religious tradition is such that it permits educational enterprise only up to a certain point, or only directed towards certain ends, this is a weak economy in which the stimulus of explanation and exploration with young people cannot revive the richness of the tradition. A new form of educational economy is needed if the ambivalent relationship between religion and education is to be resolved. There appear to be three different kinds of transaction in a flourishing educational economy, each of which is capable of enriching and strengthening both the intellectual tradition of the religion and its educational commitment.

Educational economy applied to individual teachers

A strong educational economy can strengthen the influence and freedom of individual teachers. A good example of this is in the autobiographical testimony of Clare Richards, a Roman Catholic teacher of RE whose theology is transformed by being an educator. Not only does her own theology change, but her potential to change her own church, to challenge its injustices locally, is made stronger by her ability to ask questions and set people thinking. Richards gives many examples of how her understanding of the church, the sacraments and the truth of the incarnation are made more profound and radicalized by her contact with children and young people.[13]

How is this transaction possible? Jerome Bruner, reflecting on learning as a personal act of meaning, argues that reflection leads individuals not necessarily to new insights and information, and not necessarily to any ontologically pure definition of their own selves, but to a conceptual self, a notion of one's own personhood as authored by the learner.[14] We can interpret the commitment of the learner and teacher to a conceptual self as being a transaction in the educational economy of a community, because it parts with one notion of the teacher as knowledge giver, and buys something considered more valuable.

Bruner warns against the failure to make this transaction. To fail to invest in the conceptual self is to reduce teaching to mere information-giving, which 'cannot deal with anything beyond the well-defined and arbitrary',[15] and – by implication – in RE terms, is highly unfitted for dealing with ambiguity, layered meanings, metaphors and complexity. A pedagogy that restricts itself to information-giving is 'a monkey in the British Museum, beating out the problem by a bone-crushing algorithm or taking a flyer on a risky heuristic'.[16] That behaviour, the reduction of all questions of human existence to matters of measurement alternating with ill-informed, undisciplined personal interpretation, characterizes the lives of those individuals who have not dared to invest in a daring pedagogical transaction, and the communal lives of those religious traditions whose educational economies are poor.

Thus, for a teacher who is also a learner, also committed to continuing growth and change, the transactions of teaching and learning strengthen the internal economy of the teacher as someone in charge of their own destiny, writing their own life.[17] In the teaching profession, much teacher autobiography contains narratives of themselves as heroic and creative individuals up against a rigid bureaucratic or standards-obsessed system. But it is also possible to see autobiography as transformation through renewed self-construction. One teacher saw autobiography as 'the search for a key which had the power to unlock not only a library bookcase, but my whole future. I am sure there are other teachers desperately searching for their own special keys. Despite the odds stacked against them, they should take heart.'[18] The sense of freedom engendered by this communicates itself to the subject matter, to learners and colleagues.

Educational economy applied to religious communities and organizations

Where religious communities operate in state-maintained school sectors, they are expected to uphold the law and to enact educational and other policies in relation to children. In the English system, one example of such an expectation was the Every Child Matters policy,[19] based on a definition of well-being that included personal, medical, academic, social and economic measures. Religious communities and organizations working in the education sector would, therefore, be under an obligation to take this definition, and its thinking, into their own system and work with it effectively. The Every Child Matters policy (ECM) is discussed by Muslim educator Maurice Irfan Coles, whose work[20] treads delicately a path between loyalty to English Muslim communities and institutions, such as the Muslim Council of Britain, and commitment to ECM. The delicacy of this path is seen in Coles' acknowledgement of physical and mental health issues in the English Muslim community, triggered by internal cultural factors such as family honour or *izzat*, consanguinity and the lure of criminal or terrorist underworlds. On these issues Coles is prepared to argue that ECM should come first as a priority above any urge to leave the Muslim community's internal culture unchallenged: he gently chides and encourages the Muslim community to try harder to change its structures and attitudes. Coles fails to drive his argument as far as it will go; he does not address the lack of opportunity amongst young Muslims to discuss theology as distinct from memorizing it, and attributes bad practice to culture rather than the heart of faith.[21] Nevertheless, his work serves as an example of a transaction that can change a religious community as a whole, by feeding into it a policy programme that creates a challenge and a dissonance.

Willingness to acknowledge the dissonance is the key transaction in this aspect of an educational economy. We can contrast Coles' willingness with the caution and avoidance adopted by many organizations and communities. An unwillingness to give offence to religious authorities, or a fear of controversy in the classroom, may lie at the roots of the avoidance. In the Church of England's 2001 review of its own schools and educational enterprise, *The Way Ahead*,[22] Lord Dearing reported evidence that church schools were at the centre of the church's mission to the nation, alongside parishes. The review urged that if children were not coming to the church, the church must go to them.[23] The report did not grapple with how children as learners might change the church, other than a brief mention of the need to reassess the training of clergy and the work of parishes.[24] A decade later, the same church reaffirmed its commitment to schools and made two recommendations that would spread an educational economy to other parts of church life.[25] At the launch of the later report, several church members spoke in support and expressed frustration that the church was not thinking educationally. A similar weakness is reported in the mainly Roman Catholic study, *Does the Church Really Want Religious Education?*,[26] in which the range of answers offered includes a heavily qualified affirmative, only 'of a kind and to a degree'.[27] However, a more open position is seen in the current senior educational representative of the Church of England, who argues that the church needs to make children's voices heard politically and educationally.[28]

The better choice is for religious communities, minority and majority, to allow policy initiatives such as ECM, equality measures and young people's voice to be the occasion of questioning their own positions, motives and rationale. In doing so, a community embarks on the same journey of enquiry that is required of the learner, and this may lead to shifts in collective understanding.

Educational economy applied to theology and interpretation

So far we have touched on examples of what might transform individuals and organizations in a strong educational economy. What might happen to the content of their traditions, the treasure of theological content and hermeneutics to which they are committed, and which they attempt to transmit? For many theological traditions, these theologies are deposits in the intellectual vault, which must not be changed and can only be handed on. However, is it possible that educational endeavour, as well as changing individuals and organizations, can also influence the theologies themselves and the way they are interpreted? For a theological tradition and community to have a strong educational economy, in other words to be educationally competent and trustworthy, it is essential that the treasure be taken out of the vault. The intellectual wealth grows if the heart of theological content is also treated educationally.

The mechanisms by which this educational treatment of the heart of theology may or may not happen can be exemplified in different interpretations of the parable of the good Samaritan (Luke 10: 25–37), a story much used in RE. In eastern orthodoxy the parable becomes an allegory: the 'certain man' is humanity, 'falling among thieves' is sin, the priest and the Levite are Judaism, the Samaritan is Christ, the inn is heaven. The allegorical interpretation works poorly with primary children for a number of reasons, usually connected with their distance from the scene of the story, and also their inability to lift the heavy weight of doctrine that is being pressed down on the structure of the events. The application of a doctrine of salvation to this story, to Western ears, seems cumbersome. The insertion of a supercessionalist theory to suggest the replacement of the Jews in God's favour is unsavoury and, when questioned, improbable: why would the gospel writers have the Christ of the Messianic secret engage in such allegorical theory-weaving about himself? Why would he do so in answer to a question 'who is my neighbour?'

Western interpretations are quite different, normally focusing on a moral, rather than theological-allegorical reading of the story. The dominant interpretation focuses on the moral example of a single act of kindness, an act committed by a member of a racial and religious group despised by the original hearers of the story. In RE, pupils are usually invited to see the risks taken by the Samaritan to help his enemy, and encouraged to see parables within their own time and place: the Samaritan as biker, drug dealer or person with AIDS, for example. While the content of meaning offered is more accessible, there is still a one-dimensionality to the use of the parable. A structured opportunity to interrogate the motives of the storyteller, or the wisdom of following the implied moral message – helping apparently helpless people on lonely, dangerous roads – is rarely opened up.

However, our interest here is not so much in the interpretations of the parable itself as in the influence of pedagogical thinking on theology. When a competent teacher observes that a particular religious interpretation strategy does not work well with children, or that it tends to seal off certain avenues of questioning, two courses of action appear: to persist with the interpretation, or to stop and change direction in the classroom. The former strategy requires the teacher to believe that the official interpretation is true and must be conveyed, overriding any concern about its inappropriateness for the learners. The latter effectively asks the religious community to think again about its interpretation, and thus begins a process of theological change and development. Whether this questioning and change only happens inside the teacher's mind, or takes place in live interrogation of the text and the sanctioned hermeneutic, the effect is still the same: official theology has been forced, in one small instance, to change its rules. Once the wall is breached, further instances and other theologies might also be challengeable.

Another example is the encounter between Jesus and the Syro-Phoenician woman (Mark 7:24–30). By being a woman and of mixed race, the central subject of this story is doubly disadvantaged; her approach and request to Jesus seems weighted against her. The commonest official interpretation offered in schools is the 'test of faith'. The woman asks Jesus to heal her daughter, who is possessed by an unclean spirit; he refuses, comparing her to a dog, to test her faith; she, full of faith, persists; he relents, and tells her that her daughter is healed. Although he does not actually praise her faith (as he does, for example, with the Roman centurion), the implication is that he was testing her faith, found it strong and so rewarded her. To a pupil learning the skills of questioning and interpreting stories, this reading is full of unsatisfactory strains. Why does he test her faith in this way, when he does not apply this test to others who ask? Why does he add in a racial slur, and how is that supposed to build up her faith? What would he have done if she had given up? Would and should his desire to heal her daughter be conditional upon her answers? If so, what value is to be placed on healing as a sign of the kingdom? In short, enquirers into this story's most commonly used official interpretation are asking: how can we accommodate this theology with our own discomforting questions about it? Are the pedagogical rules such that this is the only interpretation, ethically dubious though it seems to us?

A modern twist on the parable is that Jesus employed a racial and sexual slur deliberately in order to provoke the woman into a more determined appeal. Those who use this interpretation have not adequately explained how an insult is supposed to improve motivation – a notion that most teachers would emphatically disavow, especially if they are working with disadvantaged groups.

An additional liberationist twist is that Jesus did not even know his own prejudices, but was merely behaving as most Jewish males would at that time; that she radicalized him by her defiance; that his healing of her daughter came about because, in a social sense, she healed him of his attitude; that the reign of God can be understood as changing individuals but also changing God. When we get into this hermeneutic territory, further questions could come up: how come the son of God has prejudices? How come the Almighty needs challenging and healing? How are our own perceptions about race and sex, and our own valuing of equality, impacting on our sense of meaning in this story? Again we see that the questioning gaze of the young presents challenges to the tradition's approved and improvised ways of interpreting and presenting itself to the world: but at least we see, in the third interpretation, that theology has been goaded into creativity and a measure of realism.

Several stories in other traditions could be subjected to the same treatment. What of the violence done to Ganesh, apparently by his father? What of the existence of caste, the treatment of untouchables and its relationship to Sanatan Dharma? What of the Guru's treatment of animals at the inauguration of the Khalsa? What of polygamy and covert homosexual practice in Islam?

Any theological tradition with a strong educational economy can learn, from these and comparable examples, the paradox that to continue it must change, and to save its theological wealth it must speculate in the educational market. This theological realization feeds back into the theology as a result of educational encounters. Thus a theological tradition starts to learn, or learns again what it had forgotten, that there cannot be one approved meaning to stories; stories, symbols and rituals diminish in value if one official meaning is adhered to, and they can accrue if multiple meanings, including new meanings derived from transactions with young enquirers, are included.

Traditions can also learn that their writings and moral codes are conditioned by culture, gender and geography. For example, many scriptures carry narratives of racial, sexual and religious superiority, and celebrations of threatened or actual violence, without often questioning them. Their many hermeneutic strategies for accommodating this fact do not very often include the possibility that the scripture meant what it said, was morally wrong then and remains so now. Theological traditions can learn to adopt this change in hermeneutic strategy without risking their own destruction. They change best when subjected to open questioning and the insights of learners. They must change if they wish to remain alive and authoritative.

What might a strong educational economy look like?

There is a pressing need for conceptual development and narration of the idea of a strong educational economy enriching religious or philosophical communities. Most religious communities involved in state-based RE have intentionally ensured that the influence is all one way, from them to the school. In the English system, Standing Advisory Councils on RE (SACREs) have drawn some local religious leaders into an educational milieu, but (as discussed in Chapter 5) the transactions have mainly been to ensure that religions are represented to their satisfaction. SACREs lack the power to challenge religious communities to think educationally. Religions must intervene in their own cultures to make this happen at the three levels of transaction discussed here – individuals, organizations and theological ideas – and there is a need to collect more evidence. Meanwhile, however, we can imagine what a religious or ideological community might be like if it had a strong commitment to educational principles that influenced and fed back into its own people, institutions and theology. How would we describe the behaviour of such a community?

Generally, religious and philosophical communities with strong educational economies would be discursive, democratic and dynamic. Individual leaders and members would discuss and question together, communally and intergenerationally. Progress would be encouraged through questioning. The art of spiritual autobiography for individuals and communities would be encouraged. Institutions would be ahead of society on human rights and equalities. Young people's voice would be a regular part of decision making and service. Resources, such as ministry, buildings and authority structures, would be responsive to major issues. Those in ministry would have a highly developed sense of themselves as professionals, accountable, permanently developing and learning.

Dynamism would affect not only the conversations and decisions of these communities, but also their treatment of their theological tradition. It is in this regard that most religious traditions would find it most difficult, and yet also most rewarding, to change. Instead of seeing their theological tradition as a permanent, inert deposit to be saved and handed on to passive recipients, they would see each generation as dynamically adding to theology, merely by their existence, as well as their active questioning. The central insights of a tradition would not be reduced to propositions; understanding would be layered, complex, changing; the art of autobiography would be both a discipline and a measure for complex understanding. Narratives of how a tradition has changed, how understandings have changed, from one generation to another would be celebrated. The possibility of disagreement within a tradition would not be crushed by authority structures, nor would the reality of disagreement be ignored by an ethic of tolerance; instead, forums of explanation would continue to work at diverse meanings. Traditions would use such forums to continue working at understanding, to save themselves from collapsing into dualities of rigid orthodoxy and flaccid personal opinion. The complexity and intellectual challenge of traditions would not be hidden away, nor would it be diluted; questions would be used to deepen understanding. Among the many questions central to the promoting of this economy would be: How did we, as a tradition, reach this formula of belief? How did we evolve this ritual? How have we understood this story, that example? What in our present context helps us to add to our tradition's understanding and use of these things? Have some of our beliefs, practices or values become an impediment? How can we continue to remake our tradition?

To some attenders at today's gurdwaras, mandirs, mosques, synagogues, churches and chapels, these questions may appear strange; they may provoke reactions into stances of distinctiveness, firm adherence to tradition, and reliance on tried and tested formulations of the faith. The apparent strangeness of the questions, and the sense of deracination and disorientation they may induce, is evidence of how very far such communities are from being committed to learning, how weak their educational economies have become.

If religious communities feel confident enough in their tradition and their journey to open themselves to learning and questioning; if they take as their models the most creatively discursive, democratic and dynamic aspects of constructivist educational theory and practice; if they begin behaving like the best of educational communities, rather than expecting educational communities to behave like religious ones; these steps would dramatically change the relationships between religious communities and educational endeavour, and would change, but not lose, the distinctive presence of religious insight in the midst of society.

If an educational economy fails: the tyranny of facts and opinions

Religious or other ideological communities whose educational economy has failed – in other words, those belief communities that have closed themselves to most or all forms of critical open enquiry – create a contagion of debt which affects the intellectual life of other belief systems.

Any religion or ideology that divides the world of ideas starkly into truth and falsehood – as, for example, most fundamentalisms do – has set an epistemological lock on information about itself, and has thereby controlled discourses about itself and its opponents, in ways which are anti-educational. Discourses proposing that *either* Jesus was the son of God *or* he was a fraud, that *either* Muhammad is the seal of the prophets *or* there is nothing but relativism and polytheism, are all too prevalent in the economies of religious communities, and they create dispositions towards particular kinds of teaching. The discourses are designed to drive hearers ineluctably to set conclusions, and even if dealt with by a teacher who takes care to attempt objectivity, these discourses skew the discussion and exploration. They create, in the minds of some learners, a binary distinction between knowability and unknowability, between fact and opinion – a distinction which need not exist, and which subverts a critical education.

The binary distinction is unfortunately lent credibility by neo-conservative educational thinking which encourages a knowledge-based approach to the curriculum. In England, the Secretary of State for Education, Michael Gove, has endorsed the idea of a curriculum based on facts.[29] Justified as a desire to be less prescriptive, his apparent preference is for a curriculum that simply lists the knowledge to be taught: 'I just think there should be facts.'[30] In an interview, Gove used the word 'facts' four times, and the words 'understanding' and 'skills' not at all. In the United States, the Hersch-inspired core knowledge programme constructs a curriculum from the same basic building blocks.[31] Thus learning is reduced to knowledge, and knowledge to facts. There are no forms of knowledge that are not facts: anything that cannot be a fact must be a 'mere' opinion, relegated to a less important field. As an assumption, this creates epistemological conditions inimical to critical learning. In Pierre Bourdieu's phrase, 'the very structure of the field in which the discourse is produced and circulates'[32] makes some discourses possible and others illegitimate, and this is a form of censorship.

Can we imagine what a curriculum for RE would look like if it were composed of facts? Can we construct a pedagogy based on the communication of religious facts, and would such a pedagogy have integrity? Statements of 'fact', iterations and reiterations of 'knowledge' can become timelessly self-evident, self-replicating and unquestionable, turning them into truths.[33] If we were to apply this to teaching, for example, about the resurrection as a 'fact' for Christians, or nirvana as a 'fact' for Buddhists, we could see the problem developing. The problem is further compounded by Gove's assumption that a curriculum should arrange facts in order – 'a logical sequence by which facts accumulate'.[34] Would the sequence in RE be shaped by a young learner's growing ability to hold and wield ideas, or – more likely – by a supposed order determined by the internal logic of the discipline? For example, would RE first cover the Old Testament, then the New? Would it take the Gospels before Acts, Hinduism before Buddhism? In doing so, it would already have set the epistemological locks on learners' minds, predetermining the way the subject is gradually constructed in their understanding.

It should be acknowledged that all curricula are forms of selection, elevating certain kinds of knowledge and repressing others,[35] and that all forms of officially approved speech or literature are ideological.[36] In this sense, some form of organized control of educational processes is inescapable. But this does not render all forms of control equal in their influence. The teaching of 'facts' in RE would be particularly baneful because it would create advantages for those who want their own religious truths to be taught as facts, for those who want a continuation of the flawed phenomenological project of claimed objectivity and for those who wish to minimize young people's experience of debate and critical thought for political reasons.

The teaching of RE as facts necessarily precludes the possibility of debate. As a result it also, necessarily, curtails the possibility of learners' participation and autonomy within their own learning. This would be an impoverishment of educational possibility, offering no place to articulacy and empowerment. Whilst posing as a form of academic rigour, facts are a denial of the capacities upon which academic rigour is founded, and therefore a denial of the idea of democratic education.

As in any totalitarian system, the learner confronted with 'facts' is permitted only two possible responses: quiescence or revolt. Quiescence leads to success in school and career terms; it creates rewarding relationships with authority figures and nurtures a strong sense of institutional belonging, which in turn encourages more conformity; it delivers good grades, smoothes the path to university and the probability of economic success. Quiescence also embeds, reinforces and rewards habits of valuing security above truth and duty above integrity, and the suppression of any disposition towards curiosity and enquiry, criticality, debate or controversy – or at least, it places unspoken but clearly sensed limits on such habits. Quiescent states of mind are ideal for preserving both religious authority structures and the liberal project to avoid difficult questions about diversity and truth – questions which we must face, and teach young people to face. Conversely, revolt leads to the opposite of all of these: rejection, exclusion, failure, poverty. Is there a fear of young people being empowered to think for themselves? Is there a hope that 'facts' will create a subservient workforce? Is there a fear of democratic values themselves?

Facts are a way of embedding certainty. They are a pedagogical fundamentalism, paralleling religious or ideological fundamentalisms in the sense that they create a closed system that cannot be questioned, and create reaction. Within the closed system are facts that are truths; outside are opinions that are relative. Both facts and opinions would escape critical scrutiny, the first because they are privileged and the second because they are considered unimportant. This would lead to a form of RE potentially far worse for learners than at present: easier to teach, but very clearly lacking in integrity in academic terms, and impoverishing learning.

Conclusion

Any religious or ideological community whose educational economy is failing – whose attitude to learning has been degraded to units of 'fact', 'truth' or 'information' to be transmitted – will find, in the neo-conservative project, a useful partner. In the same way, any reactionary educational policy that wishes to diminish learning to 'facts' will find fundamentalist or reactionary religious communities useful and attractive partners.

And conversely, any belief community that prizes insight, complexity, questioning and change as signs of spiritual and intellectual life, and any government interested in education as an expression of democracy, no matter how imperfect, will wish to make a priority of enabling those who might wish to ask: 'Is it so? Is this information placed before me reliable?' It is to allow those voices to break forth, in learners of all ages, that a successful and honest model of RE needs all religious and ideological communities to permit themselves to be influenced by critical education – to infuse the spirit of learning into their theologies, institutions and individuals. Our portrait of a future model that addresses these challenges is presented in the final chapter.

Chapter 9

Between education and catastrophe
The futures of RE

Mark Chater and Clive Erricker

Opening story

We share the train carriage as strangers. Opposite me sits a young man listening privately to his music, which he changes periodically. He is wearing a t-shirt advertising a sport. The logo on his bag is Animal. He wears designer glasses and has a pierced ear. On his hand is an ink mark, showing that he has been stamped into a club. The several forms of identity, visual and aural, that he has chosen for his journey say something about him.

Across the aisle from him sits a middle-aged Muslim woman in full body and face covering, with two small children. I can only speculate as to her personality: there are no clues, other than the one massive statement of self-incarceration.

How much thinking have they both done about their choice of clothes and accessories? What do the other occupants – silent, avoiding eye contact – make of them? Has anyone in the carriage got something to say about identity dressing? What if we strangers were to start a conversation with each other about the significance of the clothes, logos and accessories we choose, what we want them to say about us, their economic and cultural provenance? What if everyone in school had the chance to ask these questions?

Many in the carriage know what they think and feel about the Muslim woman. Those who took RE at school will perhaps have considered and evaluated the beliefs, practices and artefacts of her religion. Even so, they cannot really know her, and she will not allow herself to be known. But very few will have had similar opportunity to study critically the equivalent beliefs, practices and artefacts of globally marketed identity retail. So we all continue our journey in silence, as strangers.

Introduction

Religious education is caught in conflicting currents. Religious communities, struggling between their own various impulses of resurgent violent extremism, lower-intensity resistance to modernity and creative accommodations to it, have ever greater difficulty in defining themselves. The arrival of democracy, universal education and information technology has changed the ownership of religions such that their wisdom and insights can change hands, and change content, as rapidly as any other information.[1] The education industry is similarly pulled in different directions, sometimes compelled to obey reactionary or populist instructions, at others called to innovate with new knowledge about children's learning, and always endeavouring to keep a school stable. Multiple futures await education: narratives of radical uncertainty and assumptions that the future is highly problematic compete with attempts at business as usual, undermining teachers' capacity to think creatively about the long-term development of their art.[2]

Our current model of RE is vulnerable, partly because it has been living between these two conflicted and disputed forces, religion and education, for several decades, reaching provisional accommodations between them. The accommodations have been both on an intellectual level (for example, phenomenology and critical realism) and on the level of practical policy (for example, SACREs and agreed syllabuses). RE has survived for a long time in this confused zone, presenting itself sometimes as an adjunct to religions and at others as an educational discipline. However, over time the unease generated by this liberal accommodation has grown both within the RE community and in the wider, interlinked communities of other subjects and educationalists. The survival strategy has now failed because the contrasting paradigms of religion and modernity are moving away from each other, albeit in complex and contradictory ways, and because the global economic crisis and radical systemic changes in the UK's education system have swept away the policy consensus around RE and the local machinery that kept it alive. The current paradigm of RE is waning, cannot be further defended, and must be replaced.

Paradigms in tension

This moment in RE's history is ambiguous and troubling for many who have committed their efforts to the subject. On the one hand, some see decades of carefully built consensus buckling under theoretical strain, while the practical progress RE has made, in numbers of students and in curriculum recognition, starts to fall away. They regret these losses and wonder if RE will ever gain a position of theoretical coherence and educational self-assurance. On the other hand, there are those who admit that the damage RE is currently sustaining has internal as well as external causes, and see this as an opportunity to resolve, for the long term, the so-far incomplete project of theorizing and enacting a proper purpose of the subject we presently call RE. Beneath this resolution lies the task of examining the relationships between religious forms of knowledge and modernity.

Children and young people are witnesses to this moment, albeit with limited understanding of its theoretical and political detail; but they see it close up in classrooms, and in the changeable and at times inconsistent ways in which knowledge paradigms are used in RE and the rest of the curriculum. They are acute observers of the hierarchy of subjects, and know when a subject is poorly regarded or marginalized in their school. They witness the way in which RE tries, at times, to objectify and problematize religion, claiming objectivity yet forgetful of its own cultural inheritance (see Chapters 4 and 5); equally, they witness the ways in which RE attempts to rehabilitate some forms of religious knowledge in a modernist world – in Habermas's phrase, to 'salvage some old truth or other'.[3] Some learners find this epistemological mixture confusing; others find it dishonest.

In a constantly changing world, in which paradigms are in tension with one another due to advances in knowledge, we believe that children and young people need to be able to develop an understanding of why this has come to be and how it affects their generation. Often enough this need extends to their parents and teachers too. What has happened to the old forms of religious knowledge, and why do they feel different from other subjects? What has been happening to RE? How does one negotiate this complexity without withdrawing into a perspective that, whilst impoverished, offers at least some semblance of certainty? The latter is what epistemological fundamentalists do, whether religious or scientific.

One way to recognize the difficulty of this moment is with recourse to Derrida's analysis of the idea of the pharmakon.[4] Derrida refers to the passage in Plato's *Phaedrus* where the inventor–god Theuth presents his invention of writing to the Great God–King Thamus. Theuth proclaims it as a pharmakon for memory and wisdom. In Greek *pharmakon* means either cure or poison. Theuth offers writing as a cure or remedy, promoting memory and wisdom. Thamus perceives it as a poison, because writing will stop the exercise of memory and create forgetfulness.[5] Derrida points out that therefore a pharmakon is an undecidable (as an example of new knowledge and what the value of its effect might be). An undecidable becomes decided through dispute over the value of its effect. In the contemporary world there are several pharmakons: the splitting of the atom created new forces of energy but also the atom bomb; new medical breakthroughs create dispute between scientists and religious authorities, for example over birth control, abortion and stem cell research. Derrida's point is that new knowledge or discovery inevitably results in contention as to how its use might affect the human condition in practice. We can extend this by saying it creates a challenge to those who live within particular knowledge paradigms, because it forces them to make an evaluation of such discoveries based on the worldview they inhabit – thus it becomes a cure or a poison. The judgement is made not solely on an epistemological basis, but also on a political one. The question is whether the new discovery creates a threat to the established norms – the mores, values and authorities – and to those who live within that paradigm. This is an existential conundrum involving the politics of power and the viability of tradition and its truths. This becomes even more acute when those who hold these differing paradigms live in close proximity to each other. Globalization and technology have brought competing paradigms into virtual proximity. Such a situation creates new threats and tensions.

Generally, such pharmakon moments have particular impact on the young as they seek to navigate between old and new forms of knowledge, tradition and new influences. In education, the crucial aim must be to equip young people with the best possible tools to recognize why undecidability happens, how they and others actually have to decide, and what the possible outcomes and effects of decidability can be. Because such activity is dependent upon contextualizing new knowledge and discovery within specific worldviews, their conceptual construction and their values systems, it has to work with the materials presented by religions and philosophies, but it cannot simply represent them.

The current situation of RE embodies within itself the dispute over the pharmakon of modern and post-modern knowledge paradigms. Do these new forms of knowledge offer a cure for RE or a poison? This remains an undecidable until RE takes a decision on its stance in regard to old and new knowledge paradigms. The issue is epistemological because it decides how knowledge is handled in RE; it is also political because the power structures in and around RE determine knowledge.

RE and the new enlightenment

If the epistemological options available to teachers and young people are restricted to the usual three – pre-modernist reaction and denial, provisional modernist accommodation or caricatures of post-modernity as relativist abdication – then the pharmakon moment is wasted, and the educational project called RE is lost already. However, the force behind the original modernist enlightenment is such that it can be reconstructed: it can give the makers of knowledge fresh insights, new light to shed on the meaning of their work. In a lecture on the new enlightenment, Matthew Taylor[6] of the RSA called on knowledge makers to break out of our present, highly problematic epistemic paradigm, by re-evaluating and re-shaping the virtues and ideas of the original enlightenment. He argued that we can do this by looking to new insights into human nature. For example, in speaking of autonomy, he suggested that we ought now to make choices on the foundation of a more complex notion of the self, aware of the possibilities and frailties of human nature; we ought to question our inherited models of progress, and consider the ultimate end purpose of human beings. If the content and even the language of these suggestions is faintly reminiscent of the catechism – the frailty of human nature, the chief end of man – this should neither surprise us nor mislead us into claiming Taylor as an ally to religious certainty. His point is that the enlightenment should move beyond its own certainties, including its own certainty in brushing aside religious certainties. For those concerned with the plight of RE, his proposal is for a new way of knowing, which lifts the subject out of its present dilemmas.

The imperative facing young people is to grow up with the capacity to navigate the world, with its shifts in knowledge and meaning, and to be effective agents in it. This need has become the foremost priority because of the grave ideological, economic and environmental threats facing their generation – threats to which older forms of knowledge as certainty have been contributing forces. RE in this new context can become a form of practical philosophy: no longer would it be concerned with the dilemma of either problematizing religion or empathizing with it; instead, RE can focus on reading and interpreting the world, particularly the world of ideas and actions. The task of reading, interpreting and acting in the world is not study solely: it is also a matter of scrutiny and reconstruction. It can remake the world, and challenge the religious, philosophical and political ideas that have gained dominance in it.

In this way of understanding our subject, young people's agency in their learning would be transformed, and would become central to the enterprise. No longer would children be the recipients of a religious tradition presented as the truth – a model which confessional religious educators increasingly see as problematic; and no longer would they be random unwitting accessories in the presentation of a liberally sanitized view of religions. Instead, in this paradigm young people would become manufacturers of knowledge, working with integrity. They would be makers of morality, makers of insight, makers of change, constructing it from the ethical, religious, philosophical and ideological materials around them. This paradigm immediately lifts RE out of many of its current and most worrisome weaknesses, but also challenges many RE assumptions. For example, no longer should teachers need to be preoccupied with subject knowledge, worried about the pronunciation or meaning of words, whether to cover the head when entering a building, or how to handle a book. Instead, a good or excellent teacher would be one who works skilfully with the primary or secondary learners as they together plan and articulate their enquiries – and, if they make a mistake, they model the making of learning by clearly and humbly showing that they have learnt something. Working with a paradigm in which religious vocabulary is frequently changing and in question, a teacher's knowledge of vocabulary is less important; knowledge of the underlying religious or philosophical grammar – the conventions by which meaning is made and conveyed – becomes more central to the teacher's competence. In another example, no longer should teachers have to struggle with balancing the twin attainment targets of learning about and learning from, imperfectly serving two masters. Young people learning RE would be engaged in a single process of becoming the co-designers and co-constructors of ideological and cultural products that address their own, their community's and humanity's most pressing questions.

The task of making subsumes and transcends about/from. And no longer should RE seek to justify itself in terms of a claimed but unverifiable impact on social harmony or community cohesion: its cultural and intellectual products, made by the learners, would be visible to all.

This form of learning can be placed in perspective by reference to *bricolage*, a term coined by Claude Lévi-Strauss in *The Savage Mind*. A *bricoleur* (one who employs *bricolage*) was, in French, 'someone who works with his hands and uses devious means compared to those of a craftsman'.[7] But he goes on to apply it to mental activity and, in particular, mythical thought:

> The characteristic feature of mythical thought is that it expresses itself by means of a heterogeneous repertoire which, even if extensive, is nevertheless limited. It has to use this repertoire, however, whatever the task in hand because it has nothing else at its disposal. Mythical thought is therefore a kind of intellectual '*bricolage*' – which explains the relation which can be perceived between the two.[8]

For Lévi-Strauss *bricolage* has a 'mythopoetical nature' which 'can reach brilliant, unforeseen results on the intellectual plane'.[9] *Bricolage* needs to be understood and interpreted on the plane of what people do with ideas. It is not simply a transfer of information, of a bank of cultural stock, to be regurgitated. Rather it suggests a re-assemblage or remaking of things from the cultural legacy available. Not content with merely re-assembling the past, the *bricoleur* reconstructs something new from the materials of the past – its ideas, values and institutions. Learning means entering a dialectic between those worldviews inherited from the past, or constructed in the recent past, and the learner's experience of the present. The dialectic gives new life to the heritage of stories, myths and truths, and at the same time enlightens and liberates the learner with new knowledge.[10] In this way of learning, knowledge is not an inert deposit of facts, nor a complete body of truth: it is a living thing, a freshly made cultural product, constantly being re-made in the hands and minds of the learners.

In many highly successful primary schools, this type of constructivist approach is already in operation. School inspectors found it to be a key characteristic of outstanding primary schools to be that their 'development of good learning habits, with many opportunities to find things out for themselves'.[11] The habit of questioning, of planning and carrying out investigations together, is a particularly important characteristic in the teaching of sciences, history and geography. So this model, while a revolutionary step for some RE teachers, merely implies stepping into models of good teaching and learning that have already been shown to have success and integrity. The difficulty of this step for some RE teachers highlights their distance from the rest of the curriculum and the low priority they place on learning in RE as distinct from presenting religions.

By way of illustration, let us imagine a primary class in which the story of the good Samaritan is being taught. But in announcing this we have already betrayed the spirit of the new constructivist model, by placing content before questions. In this class, the teacher poses the question to pupils aged 9: How can we understand each other better in our community, and help each other more? This is an enquiry, crossing different subjects, that will last several weeks. As part of the enquiry, the teacher wants a story that engages the 9-year-olds in challenging views about others – a story that is material from one major religious tradition, containing many potential truths about how we see others. She therefore comes to the good Samaritan, not as staple religious fare with only one meaning, but as a problem posed to the children and the characters in the story itself. The Jericho Road: why was it dangerous, and what streets are like that in our area? Stopping and helping someone: why is it sometimes difficult, or even unwise, to help a person who looks and feels different? Improving a community: is it done by one single act of kindness? Give your suggestions to the innkeeper. Thus – borrowing from Martin Luther King – we can see how the use of a story becomes a transformative piece of cultural and moral making:

> It is collective local action that will transform the Jericho Road, and it is the bonds between localities that will make sure this is not an isolated right won by the few, but a control-shift that genuinely enables people.[12]

The present RE curriculum contains many stories, sayings, rituals, practices and objects that could be placed in the service of dynamic enquiries leading to the making of something. It also leaves out many stories and teachings which could be similarly used, but are not, because they are uncomfortable. But these materials will not be used in the same way, and not for their own sake. Many RE syllabuses currently use – or over-use – the story of the good Samaritan. Very few use the story of the workers in the vineyard, because it disrupts the underlying strategy that religions must be presented as consistent with our contemporary notions of fairness. Yet that story also is material from past paradigms that can be offered to the young *bricoleur* and made into new knowledge.

Pedagogical and structural proposals for the subject we currently call RE

In Chapter 3 we discussed the existing 'importance statement' for RE taken from the 2004 framework and its successors – a brief glimpse of the subject's educational rationale and purpose, the first step in defining its pedagogy. If the kind of subject we are now proposing were to have its own importance statement, what would it say? A provisional and imperfect attempt follows below: it tries to observe the requirements of pedagogy set out in Chapter 3, by saying something about the world and the delineations of the subject. In addressing the pedagogical rules of engagement, it places a process of knowledge-making – composed of enquiry, decision and action – centre-stage, and says very little about the content that will furnish these enquiries. It imposes no hierarchies of content, and only one value, that of truthfulness in enquiry. It hints at a model of student progress. Instead of being written in the abstract, this importance statement is addressed to the learners themselves, as a response to their questions about why they are studying this subject.

> You are growing up in a world that is complicated, changeable, reward-ing and dangerous. To understand this world, interpret it and act effec-tively and wisely in it, you need to understand and use ideas. People's ideas about life, the things they believe to be right and wrong, make a big difference to the world, sometimes for better, sometimes for worse. In this subject we study ideas and values, and we use them to try making a better world. For example: how well do we behave? Who decides what good behaviour is? Who makes the rules and laws? Are the rules and laws fair, and fairly applied? What do some of the great philosophies and religions tell us about life and how to live? What would we like to change, and how can we set about doing it? What does this new knowledge tell us about behaviour and rules?
>
> In this subject, adults will work with you to ask these questions and many others, helping you to find the big ideas that have shaped your world, and to use those ideas in making answers that you can use in your life, in your family, community and worldwide. Ideas can be safe or dangerous; values can be good or bad; they can change. Beliefs about the nature of our identity and our human existence on the planet, about truth and falsehood, freedom, equality and wealth, about God and each other, about our rules and how they are made, can help us to make decisions wisely and act effectively – or they can lead us to suffering, fear and destruction. In this subject you will be trying, as truthfully as you can, to find and make answers – even though that is sometimes complicated and difficult. You can change your mind, agree or disagree. You can learn by asking questions, understanding beliefs and deciding on actions. You can make progress by looking back at your questions, beliefs and actions, facing the consequences and asking deeper questions. It is part of human nature to ask questions and seek answers on meaning, purpose and value. To become better at this is to become more human.

Objections aplenty may be made to such a subject, most of them premised on a fear that it would fail to deliver on what RE presently claims to offer. First, it might be said that it abandons the study of religion or religions. The statement clearly advertises questions about God, meaning and identity, but it does not explicitly encompass an ambition to analyse religions or empathize with them. The highly problematic nature of the theoretical grounding of that study has already been discussed in Chapters 4 and 5. By stopping short of a promise to study them objectively, we avoid many difficulties. By forbearing to claim to be promoting positive attitudes to religion and diversity, we prepare the ground for a project whose success or failure can be proven. In this enquiry model, it will be legitimate to study any religion, philosophy or belief system systematically, but this would be for a declared purpose free from the grandiose claims of objectivity or social engineering. Part of the declared purpose would be that the enquiry leads to action: for example, engaging over several weeks with the question 'Can the West discover the meaning of Islam – and if so, how?' contributes to the making of new knowledge and the changing of both religion and culture. Or, for another example, taking the question 'What is the Christian church's position about money, and does it reflect the gospel?' would enable learners to grapple with the dilemmas, compromises and hypocrisies of institutions. But this subject would not be confined to questions about religions. It would also attend critically to the values ruling the way many people live, for example by having pupils ask 'Why does advertising on TV make us want things?' or 'What were the beliefs that made Bertrand Russell face a prison sentence?' No belief systems would be out of bounds in this subject unless the asking of questions about them posed dangers to children. The current hierarchies of content, and the territorialism that makes some people rule out the study of non-religious worldviews, would be gone.

Second, it may be objected that this new thing is not a proper discipline, merely a purposeless meander through wildly divergent questions. It might be dismissed as a blend of RE, citizenship and some parts of PSHE together with some politics and philosophy. It might be deemed entirely inappropriate as not part of the traditional canon of subjects taught in school. Those who would discount as illegitimate any subject that is not a pure discipline must be prepared also to eject RE as it stands now, together with design and technology, physical education, geography and perhaps some others. Whether any subject that is a combination of disciplines can properly be in the school curriculum is a matter of public debate, but the more important question is not whether a subject *is* a discipline but whether it *has* a discipline. Current RE, as we argued in Chapter 3, does not have a discipline; indeed it suffers from an undisciplined competition between several, with no resolution of their relative importance or relation to each other: critical biblical study or study of religious truth, personal development or social science, with neither the teachers nor the pupils knowing the intellectual rules and how to succeed in the subject. RE is an uneasy coalition. The new subject will be a disciplined set of enquiries into questions of power and truth, certainly in fields as diverse as religion, politics and philosophy, but in all those fields the enquiry follows intellectual rules that are recognizable and cognate.

Third, the accusation of relativism may be made, in that the statement fails to speak of promoting values (other than truthfulness[13]). Those making such an accusation, if assembled together, would next have the task of itemizing the values they want the subject to promote, followed by the realization that their list is growing impossibly long, and finally the excitement of arguing with each other about which values are most important and which should be left out, and how tolerance of different values should be squared against the values themselves. Then they would face the challenge of wondering how a subject can inculcate values. They might read Tom Lickona[14] and discover that exhortation alone does not transmit values. Our claim for this new subject is modest, promoting only one value through practising it repeatedly in enquiries. Yet our scope for engagement with many living values, for understanding their influence and shaping them to make new knowledge in communities, is almost limitless. Thus we would be making theological, philosophical and moral agents of all our learners.

Fourth might be the point that it fails to promote the English heritage of Christianity through proper attention to the historical absorption of Christian institutions, language, rituals and laws deriving from them. This is often advanced as a defence of current RE, although very rarely in official documents. The heritage may be promoted because people feel it is valuable, or under threat, or simply worth knowing about. Because our new subject turns aside from any claim or attempt to influence young people's attitudes except in regard to truthfulness, it will not intentionally set out to teach them how to love the English heritage, or that of any country or continent.

Lastly, some may fear that this subject would be inaccessible for early years and some primary children. We believe the very opposite to be the case, namely that very young children learn vigorously by asking questions and making things. Professional and scholarly studies of good practice with children aged 3 to 11 often emphasize the importance of active learning generated by enquiry.[15] We believe that too much current RE goes against the grain of that learning, defeating itself by didacticism. Very young learners need the skilled pedagogical discipline of a teacher to frame the enquiry, furnish it with processes of gaining new knowledge and guide it towards action so that learning changes their world as well as changing the things learnt about. They are the most natural *bricoleurs*.

Our proposed subject is not RE; it goes beyond learning about and learning from; it is not philosophy, nor does it conform to the rules of philosophy for children. It is more about the grammar of insight than its vocabulary; it is unambiguously for the sake of the world, not for the religions; it offers the chance to make knowledge and change. In European, north American and secular education jurisdictions, it stands a chance of implementation because it avoids calling itself RE. In the context of the British, and particularly the English, system, it would succeed only if widely taken up by teachers from the grass roots, or by a change in the law.

It is a subject that does not need a statutory right to withdraw, unless this right applies to all parts of the curriculum; it does not need teachers to be prepared through intensive subject knowledge, so much as skilled teachers who understand the pedagogical process; it does not need SACREs, except perhaps as voluntary panels for resourcing the subject, in which case they should change their name, open their membership widely and stop writing local agreed syllabuses; it does not need legal prescriptions on the balance of Christian and other content, but would benefit from a complete embracing of the Toledo principles on openness[16] and a fearless spirit of enquiry.

And the name – religious education? At the time of writing, a change of name is widely debated amongst RE professionals. Several schools have experimented already, as they have legal freedom to do. Secondary departments of Ethics and Religion, examination courses in Philosophy and Ethics, investigations into Who We Are and What We Believe, are abounding. There is a case for moving on from the current name. The word 'education' is redundant, and the word 'religious' fails to capture all that can and should be studied. RE has become an unhelpful name, suggestive of religion qualifying education, and misleading as to the best potential and best intentions of the subject. If – and only if – the subject community embraces profound change of the kind we have argued for, it might also change its name: but this would be pointless cosmetics unless the deeper transformation in purpose and pedagogy has already taken root in the subject community.

Conclusion

Does RE have a future? All living traditions survive by evolution, changing their inner convictions and outer structures as they deem necessary. Religions are changing, although their accommodation to modernity, democracy and new knowledge paradigms is painfully slow, grudging and inconsistent. Education systems are changing rapidly, provoking crises of confidence in themselves, and discovering ways of learning that make present knowledge paradigms redundant. RE, deeply affected by both religion and education, is caught inevitably in the dynamics of this change. If RE fails to transform itself; if it clings to its doubtful rationale of objectivity, or other flawed pedagogies; if it fails to invent new structures and partnerships; if it declines to submit itself to the full accountability of young people's gaze and neglects their aspirations for the world they will inherit; then it will deserve to die.

In the RE community there are many who see this, and see something else: the power of learning to change the learner, the subject matter and the world. They understand that RE must re-engineer itself, evolving its inner convictions and outer structures for this task. If they are given freedom, they will create a future for something that is a rightful successor to RE – something that will claim the full loyalty and recognition of all who are working for a revolution in learning.

Notes

Introduction

1 R. Jackson, *Rethinking Religious Education and Plurality*, London: Routledge Falmer, 2004, pp. 4–21.
2 J. Keast, *An RE for Europe?* Birmingham: Christian Education, Resource, 2006, pp. 13–15.
3 L. Philip Barnes, ed., *Debates in Religious Education*, London: Routledge, 2012.
4 P. Clough, *Narratives and Fictions in Educational Research*, Buckingham: Open University Press, 2002; L. Richardson, *Writing: a method of inquiry research*, in N. Denzin and Y. Lincoln, eds, *A Handbook of Qualititative Research*, Thousand Oaks, Calif.: Sage, pp. 926ff.

I The global context of religion and belief

1 I use the term 'offshore capital' to denote how the accumulation of different forms of capital – financial but also political, religious, social and cultural, and educational capital – can be accumulated through it being 'offshore' in relation to democratic and international regulation as well as within it. The idea of 'offshore capital' is well known in relation to global finance and government deregulation of banks that produced the 2008 collapse and its aftermath. However, it is not so well appreciated how the term can be used to expose the way in which religions can act without sufficient restraint, or oppose democratic regulation, in relation to the accumulation of other forms of capital that threaten democracies. Therefore the idea of 'offshore capital' enables us to make more sense of the issues democratic government and democratic ethics face in a globalized world.
2 See, for example, Talal Asad, *Formations of the Secular: Christianity, Islam and modernity*, Stanford: Stanford University Press, 2003, and Peter L. Berger, 'Secularization and de-secularization' in Linda Woodhead, ed., *Religions in the Modern World*, London: Routledge, 2002, pp. 291–8.
3 Nicholas Shaxson, *Treasure Islands: Tax havens and the men who stole the world*, London: Bodley Head, 2011, p. 27.
4 Irena Maryniak, Among the old believers, *Index on Censorship*, 33 (213), 4 October, 2004, p. 49.
5 Two contrasting, but both controversial, examples can be cited here to illustrate the problem. The anti-gay Westboro Baptist Church pickets military funerals in the United States as dead soldiers return from Iraq and Afghanistan. In a case brought by the father of a dead marine the Supreme Court ruled eight to one in favour of Westboro on the basis of their constitutional right to free speech. Their activity included picketing about 200 funerals with placards and chanting rejoicing in the death of the combatants whether or not the dead soldier had been gay. This ruling overturned a previous ruling against

Westboro in the federal court, upon appeal. See E. MacAskill, 'US court allows anti-gay funeral pickets to go on', London and Manchester: newspaper, 3 March 2011, p. 24).

The second example is that of the French parliament which has banned the niqab being worn in public, in April 2011, in a bill on 'covering one's face in public places'. (see A. Chrisafis, 'Outlawed on the street, in shops, at banks, in theatres: France spells out niqab ban', London and Manchester: *Guardian* newspaper, 4 March 2011, p. 3).

6 See Kenan Malik, *From Fatwah to Jihad: the Rushdie affair and its legacy*, London: Atlantic Books, 2009, p. 18.

7 See Mohsen Kadivar, God and His guardians, *Index on Censorship*, 33 (213), 4 October 2004, pp. 64–71.

8 Sarah Maitland, In place of enlightenment, *Index on Censorship*, 33 (213), 4 October 2004, p. 8.

9 Ibid, p. 9.

10 Ibid, p. 11.

11 Ibid.

12 G. Robertson, *The Case of the Pope: Vatican accountability for human rights abuse*, London: Penguin, 2010, p. 42.

13 Ibid, p. 43.

14 Ibid, p. 79.

15 Ibid, p. 95.

16 Leonardo Boff, I sat in Leonardo's seat, *Index on Censorship*, 33 (213), 4 October 2004, pp. 31–6.

17 See, for example, Cameron supports civil partnerships in churches, http://www.christian. org.uk/news/cameron-supports-civil-partnerships-in-churches. (accessed 11 March 2011).

18 Philip Pullman, The art of reading in colour, *Index on Censorship*, 33 (213), 4 October 2004, pp. 156–63.

19 Capital here refers to different forms of capital necessary for survival and continuance. Most obviously there is economic capital: the financial capacity to implement a group's aims. But there are other forms of capital which are also of importance. Cultural capital consists of a society's ability to retain some semblance of its cultural identity. Religious capital can be understood similarly. In essence capital is what you need to preserve the identity you value. When this is eroded by other sources a minority identity has to assimilate to an overarching socio-cultural narrative: you assimilate and give up, across generations, that which you sought to preserve. How capital tensions work themselves out determines the cohesiveness of and change within the overall social fabric.

20 Sanjay Suri, *Brideless in Wembley: In search of Indian England*, Chichester: Summersdale Publishers, 2007.

21 We could also cite the view of the sociologist Richard Sennett on the failure of multiculturalism, from a UK perspective. In response to the question 'Is multiculturalism really about alienation and indifference rather than cooperation and solidarity?' He replied 'Absolutely. I've had colleagues who've traced this in the lives of schoolchildren. At six or seven, they're interleaved with each other; by the time they're 14 it's like a chemical separation – no longer speaking to people with different colour and accents. When they have to deal with each other they are at a loss.' Interview by Andrew Anthony, 'Richard Sennett Q and A', *Observer Review*, London and Manchester: Guardian Newspapers, 12 February 2012, p. 5.

22 See PM's speech at Munich Security Conference, http://www.number10.gov.uk/news/ speeches-and-transcripts/2011/02/pms-speech-at-munich-security-conference-60293 (accessed 11 March 2011).

23 Ed Husain, *The Islamist: why I joined radical Islam in Britain, what I saw and why I left*, London: Penguin, 2007.

24 Ibid, p. 73.

26 Ibid, p. 72ff.

26 Ibid, p. 29; see also Kenan Malik, *From Fatwah to Jihad*, pp. 125–30, and, on Iqbal Sacranie, head of the Muslim Council of Britain, pp. 181–2.

27 Husain, *The Islamist*, pp. 73–4.

28 Husain, Ibid, pp. 76ff.

29 University of Winchester, *MA Islamic Education definitive course document*, Winchester: University of Winchester, 2009, p. 4.

30 Ibid, p. 3.

31 Ibid.

32 Ibid, p. 4.

33 Kenan Malik, *From Fatwah to Jihad*, p. 180.

34 Ibid p. 179.

35 Particularly worrying are the sorts of events taking place in Pakistan, at the time of writing, where killings of those who have campaigned to liberalize laws on blasphemy are applauded. Salmaan Taseer and Shahbaz Bhatti were assassinated for encouraging law reform that would ensure that blasphemy did not result in a death sentence, as it presently does. In effect, their killings are symbolic of the mood in Pakistan, and elsewhere, to reject liberalism itself. See, for example, commentary on this in Nick Cohen, The Pakistan killings are not about blasphemy, *Observer* newspaper, 6 March 2011, p. 37.

36 Nabeel Yasin, A Man of his Word, *Index on Censorship*, 33 (213), 4 October 2004, pp. 79.

37 Ibid, p. 80.

38 Ibid, p. 85.

39 See Tetsuden Kashima, *Buddhism in America: The social organization of an ethnic religious institution*, Greenwood Press, 1977. For a more detailed comparison of these two groups see Clive Erricker, 'Faith Education of Children in the Context of Adult Migration and Conversion: the discontinuities of tradition' in C. Ota and C. Erricker, eds, *Spiritual Education: literary, empirical and pedagogical approaches*, Brighton and Portland: Sussex Academic Press, 2005, pp. 231–44.

40 See Clive Erricker, A Buddhist approach to alternative schooling: the Dharma School, Brighton, UK, in Philip and Glenys Woods, eds, *Alternative Education for the 21st Century*, New York: Palgrave, 2009, pp. 83–100.

41 Friedrich Schleiermacher, *On Religion: Speeches to its Cultured Despisers*, Cambridge Texts in the History of Philosophy, Cambridge: Cambridge University Press, 1996.

42 See, for example, Paul Tillich, *The Courage to Be*, Newhaven, Conn.: Yale University Press, 1952.

43 Karl Barth, *The Epistle to the Romans*, Oxford: Oxford University Press, 1968.

44 Karl Barth, *Church Dogmatics*, Edinburgh: T&T Clark, 2010.

45 E. Thornton, Protesters celebrate Christmas as judge postpones decision, London: *Church Times*, 7763, 30 December 2011, http://www.churchtimes.co.uk/content.asp?id=122516.

2 The conflicted context of education

1 For example, United Nations, *UN Declaration of Human Rights*, article 26, 1948, www.un.org/en/documents/udhr, which establishes the right to a free and compulsory education. United Nations Economic, Social & Cultural Organization, *UNESCO Declaration on Education for All*, 1990, www.un.org/en/documents/udhr. Council of Europe, *Charter on Education for Democratic Citizenship and Human Rights Education*, 2010, www.coe.int/education.

2 United Nations Office of the High Commissioner for Human Rights, *Training and Education on Human Rights Education*, nd, http://www.ohchr.org/EN/PublicationsResources/Pages/TrainingEducation.aspx.

3 See, for example, J. Holt, *Escape from Childhood*, Boston, Mass.: EP Dutton, 1974. He argues that the compulsory status of education undermines itself. J. Gatto, *Dumbing Us Down: The hidden curriculum of compulsory schooling*, Gabriola Island, Calif.: New Society Publishers, 2005, adds that compulsory entitlement creates a downward pressure on standards. I. Illich, *Deschooling Society*, London: Calder and Boyars, 1971, questioned the feasibility of universal education in capitalist societies, and called for the disestablishment of schools from state control, not for their abolition. The home schooling movement, www.education-otherwise.net, offers an alternative not available to all parents.

4 T. Oates, *Could Do Better: Using international comparisons to refine the national curriculum in England*, Cambridge: Cambridge Assessment, 2010.

5 I. Illich, in *The Mirror of the Past: Lectures and addresses, 1978–1990*, London: Marion Boyars, p. 165.

6 P. Bourdieu, The forms of capital, in J. Richardson, ed., *Handbook of Theory and Research for the Sociology of Education*, New York, Greenwood, 1986, pp. 241–58.

7 P. Bourdieu, *The Logic of Practice*, Stanford, Calif.: Stanford University Press, 1990, pp. 52–79.

8 US Department of Education, No Child left Behind Act, http://www2.ed.gov/policy/elsec/leg/esea02/pg1.html#sec1001 2001.

9 Department for Education, *Purposes of the National Curriculum*, http://www.education.gov.uk/schools/teachingandlearning/curriculum/b00199676/aims-values-and-purposes/purposes, 2011.

10 Quoted in T. Oates, *Could Do Better*, p. 5.

11 UK Department for Education, *National Curriculum Aims, Values and Purposes*, http://www.education.gov.uk/schools/teachingandlearning/curriculum/b00199676/aims-values-and-purposes/aims, 2011.

12 Department of Education and Science, *Education Reform Act*, http://www.legislation.gov.uk/ukpga/1988/40/contents, 1988, Chapter 1.

13 Department for Education, *The National Strategies*, London, DfE, 2011, http://www.education.gov.uk/schools/toolsandinitiatives/nationalstrategies. The material has been archived and some links on this site are broken.

14 R. Alexander, *Children, Their World, Their Education: Final report and recommendations of the Cambridge primary review*, London: Routledge, 2010, pp. 237, 239.

15 M. Chater, Just another brick in the wall: education as violence to the spirit, in M. Chater and C. Ota, eds, *Spiritual Education in a Divided World*, London: Taylor and Francis, 2007.

16 Department for Education, *The Importance of Teaching*, White Paper, London: DfE, 2010, pp. 29–30 and 53; Department for Education, *The Framework for the National Curriculum: A report by the expert panel for the national curriculum review*, London: DfE, 2011, p. 60.

17 T. Brighouse, Decline and fall: are state schools and universities on the point of collapse? Annual lecture to the Oxford Education Society, 16 September 2011. Oxford; University of Oxford Department of Education, 2011, pp. 3–6.

18 *Guardian*, Education Bill abolishes four quangos, 2011, http://www.guardian.co.uk/education/2011/jan/27/education-bill-abolishes-four-quangos.

19 T. Brighouse, Decline and fall, p. 4.

20 S. Cox, *The Report*, BBC Radio 4, 16 February 2012.

21 R. Pring, *Education for All: Evidence from the past, principles for the future: twelve challenges*, Oxford: Teaching and Learning Research Programme, 2011, http://www.tlrp.org/educationforall/EducationForAll.pdf p. 15.

22 UK Parliament Select Committee on Education, Think again on English baccalaureate, say MPs, London: Parliament, 28 July 2011, http://www.parliament.uk/business/committees/committees-a-z/commons-select/education-committee/news/ebac-report-substantive/.

23 Department for Education, *Criteria for Assuring High-quality Phonics Work*, London: Department for Education, http://www.education.gov.uk/schools/teachingandlearning/

pedagogy/phonics/a0010240/criteria-for-assuring-high-quality-phonic-work, 28 September 2011.

24 R. Williams, The government needs to know how afraid people are, *New Statesman*, 13 June 2011, p. 4.

25 R. Pring and M. Halstead, eds, *The Common School and the Comprehensive Ideal*, London: John Wiley and Sons, 2008.

26 T. Brighouse, Decline and fall, p. 9.

27 Z. Blackler, California, US: 'Trigger power' allows parents to call the shots, *Times Education Supplement*, 16 December 2011; see also the comments of Lord Adonis, when an education minister, in A. Adonis, We need pushy parents to improve failing schools, www.thislondon.co.uk, 25 August 2008.

28 M. Benn, *School Wars: The battle for Britain's education*, London: Verso, pp. 85–90.

29 TES (2010) Nearly half of secondary schools will consider academy status, *Times Educational Supplement*, 17 September 2010, p. 12; TES (2011b) Union warnings as LA support role disappears amid job cuts, *Times Educational Supplement*, 4 March 2011, p. 5.

30 M. Ainscow, A. Dyson, S. Goldrick and M. West, *Developing Equitable Education Systems*, Abingdon: Routledge, 2012.

31 Department for Education, *The Importance of Teaching*, White Paper, London: DfE, 2010, p. 6.

32 M. Benn, *School Wars*, p. 33.

33 TES, 16 December 2011, p. 27.

34 E. Morris, My three tests for Labour's plan, *Guardian*, 13 September 2005, www.guardian.co.uk/politics/2005/sep/13/schools.

35 Cabinet Office, *The Coalition: Our programme for government*, London: Cabinet Office, 2010, pp. 28–9.

36 S. Kent, New efficiency expo delivers real value, *ModernGov*, April/May 2011, p. 30.

37 A. Duncan, Speech to the UN Educational, Scientific and Cultural Organization (UNESCO) 4 November 2010. Common Core State Standards Initiative, http://www.corestandards.org/, accessed on 21 November 2010.

38 D. Ravitch, *The Death and Life of the Great American School System*, New York: Basic Books, 2010.

39 UK Parliament Select Committee on Children, Schools and Families, From Baker to Balls: the foundations of the education system, London: parliament, 28 April 2010, www.publications.parliament.uk/pa/cm200809/cmselect/ .../344i.pdf, para 53.

40 K. Facer, *Local Curriculum or National Curriculum: Which best serves social justice?* London: Royal Society for the Arts, www.thersa.org/projects/education/area-based-curriculum, 17 November 2011.

41 M. Young, *Local Curriculum or National Curriculum: Which best serves social justice?* London: Royal Society for the Arts, www.thersa.org/projects/education/area-based-curriculum, 17 November 2011.

42 Parents were and still are legally entitled to withdraw their child from RE (UK Parliament, School Standards and Framework Act, 1998, London: UK Parliament, section 71) and most teachers are entitled to refuse to teach it (UK Parliament, Ibid, sections 58–60). Although these rights are not much used in practice, their existence further complicates the educational credibility of the subject, and leads some school leaders to think that RE is not statutory.

43 The non-statutory national framework for RE, published jointly by the Department for Education and Employment and the Qualifications and Curriculum Authority in 2004, evolved into programmes of study for secondary pupils (2007) and primary pupils (2010). All these documents have now disappeared from official websites, but are in wide circulation in the RE community nationally.

44 Department for Education, *National Curriculum Aims, Values and Purposes*, 2011, http://www.education.gov.uk/schools/teachingandlearning/curriculum/b00199676/aims-values-and-purposes.

45 Ofsted, *Twelve Outstanding Schools: Excelling against the odds*, London: Ofsted, 2009, http://www.ofsted.gov.uk/resources/twelve-outstanding-secondary-schools-excelling-against-odds.

46 Ofsted, *Transforming Religious Education*, London: Ofsted, 2010, p. 29.

47 N. Postman, *The End of Education*, New York: Vintage Books, 1995.

48 Department for Education, *The Framework for the National Curriculum: A report by the expert panel for the national curriculum review*, London: DfE, 2011, pp. 42–3 and 60.

49 The argument that a knowledge-based approach would be catastrophic for RE is taken further in Chapter 7.

50 F. Furedi, *Wasted: Why education isn't educating*, London: Continuum, 2009, pp. 194ff.

3 The heart of the enterprise: a pedagogical problem

1 Ofsted, *Transforming Religious Education*, London: Ofsted, 2010, pp. 12–14.

2 R. Alexander, *Children, Their World, Their Education: Final report of the Cambridge primary review*, London: Routledge, 2010, pp. 302–5.

3 D. Hamilton, The pedagogic paradox, or why no didactics in England, *Pedagogy, Culture and Society*, 7 (1), 1999, pp. 135–52.

4 M. Gove, BBC Radio 4 *Today* programme, London: BBC, 20 January 2011.

5 C. Watkins, *Learning, Performance and Improvement*, London: International Network for School Improvement, London Institute of Education, 2010, p. 2.

6 In Brian Simon's essay, Why no pedagogy in England? (in B. Simon and W. Taylor, eds, *Education in the Eighties: The central issues*, London: Batsford, 1981, pp. 121–45) it is argued that the poverty of pedagogical theory in the English system is of long standing.

7 R. Alexander, *Essays on Pedagogy*, London: Routledge, 2008, p. 46.

8 J. Bruner, *The Culture of Education*, Cambridge, Mass.: Harvard University Press, 1996, pp. 44ff.

9 J. Dewey, My pedagogic creed, *School Journal*, 54, 1897, http://dewey.pragmatism.org/creed.htm p. 77.

10 J. Leach and B. Moon, *The Power of Pedagogy*, London: Sage, p. 4.

11 R. Alexander, *Children, Their World, Their Education*, p. 307.

12 R. Alexander, Ibid.

13 M. Hayward, *Christianity in Religious Education at Key Stage 3*, Coventry: Warwick University, 2007; Ofsted, *Transforming Religious Education, pp. pp12–13 and 32*.

14 C. Erricker, *Religious Education: A conceptual and inter-disciplinary approach for secondary level*, Abingdon, UK, and New York: Routledge, 2010, p. 9.

15 Qualifications and Curriculum Authority and Department for Education and Skills, *Religious Education: The National Framework*, London: QCA, 2004, p. 7.

16 National Association of Teachers of RE, What do you know about RE?, www.natre.org.uk/explore/video, 2011.

17 M. Felderhof, P. Thompson and D. Torevell, eds, *Inspiring Faith in Schools: Studies in religious education*, Aldershot: Ashgate, 2007, pp. 75ff.

18 Department for Education, *The Framework for the National Curriculum: A report by the expert panel for the national curriculum review*, London: DfE, 2011, p. 59.

19 R. Alexander, *Children, Their World, Their Education*, p. 306.

20 Experts working in confessional (mainly church school) contexts, participating in the 'Does RE work?' colloquium, were unanimous in the view that confessional Christian RE has evolved into 'supporting young people in their personal search for meaning'. V. Baumfield,

J. Conroy, R. Davis and D. Lundie, The Delphi method: gathering expert opinion in religious education, *British Journal of Religious Education*, 34 (1), Abingdon: Routledge, 2012, p. 17.

21 V. Baumfield, Editorial: Understanding the wider context: meaning and purpose in religious education, *British Journal of Religious Education*, 34 (1), Abingdon: Routledge, 2012, pp. 1–4.

22 V. Baumfield et al, The Delphi method, 2012, p. 10.

23 V. Baumfield et al, The Delphi method, 2010, p. 12.

24 M. Grimmitt, *Religious Education and Human Development*, Great Wakering: McCrimmon's, 1987.

25 Qualifications and Curriculum Authority and Department for Education and Skills, *Religious Education: The National Framework*, London: QCA, 2004, pp. 34–37. See also, Qualifications and Curriculum Development Agency, Primary Curriculum *Area of Learning: Religious education*, London: QCA, 2010, p. 7.

26 Qualifications and Curriculum Authority, *Programme of Study: Religious education*, London: QCA, 2008, p. 3 In this version the targets were referred to as learning about and from religion and belief, the addition being a reflection of the inclusion of non-religious worldviews in the content. For clarity and brevity of argument, this chapter uses the original language of the targets.

27 L. Blaylock, Assessment, in L.P. Barnes, ed., *Debates in Religious Education*, Abingdon: Routledge, 2012, pp. 235–46.

28 G. Teece, Is it learning about and from religions, religion or religious education? And is it any wonder that teachers don't get it? *British Journal of Religious Education*, 32 (2), Abingdon: Routledge/Taylor and Francis, 2010, pp. 93–104.

29 Ofsted, *Making Sense of Religion: A report on religious education in schools and the impact of locally agreed syllabuses*, London: Ofsted, 2007, pp. 34–5.

30 V. Baumfield, Pedagogy, in L.P. Barnes, ed., *Debates in Religious Education*, Abingdon: Routledge, 2012, pp. 207–8.

31 Ofsted, *Making Sense of Religion*, pp. 38–9.

32 The four skills absorbed about and from into a single pedagogy:
   a   Identify questions and define enquiries, using a range of methods, media and sources.
   b   Carry out and develop enquiries by gathering, comparing, interpreting and analysing a range of information, ideas and viewpoints.
   c   Present findings, suggest interpretations, express ideas and feelings and develop arguments.
   d   Use empathy, critical thought and reflection to evaluate their learning and how it might apply to their own and others' lives.
       (Qualifications and Curriculum Development Agency, *Primary Curriculum: Religious education*, London: QCA, 2010, p. 2.).

33 Hampshire County Council, *Living Difference*, Hampshire County Council, 2006 and 2010.

34 L.P. Barnes, Diversity, in L.P. Barnes, ed., *Debates in Religious Education*, Abingdon: Routledge, 2012, p. 73.

35 The claims of the phenomenological tradition and its contemporary successors are critically discussed by Clive in Chapters 4 and 5.

36 The confessional model is a problematic construct because it operates variably across different nations and religions. The traditional English model that pertained until the 1960s, based on biblical knowledge and cultural assumptions of Anglican hegemony, was found wanting and has long since gone (T. Copley, *Teaching Religion: Sixty years of religious education in England and Wales*, Exeter: University of Exeter Press, 2008), except that its ghost lingers in the suspicions of some opponents of RE and the fears of some apologists. Contemporary manifestations of confessionalism vary from rote learning and hate teaching (BBC, British schools, Islamic rules, *Panorama*, London: BBC, 27 November 2010, http://

www.bbc.co.uk/programmes/b00w8kwz), through the imposition of doctrinal content masquerading as lesson objectives (M-J. Martin, *Icons: A religious education programme for 11–14* (volume 1), London: Harper Collins, 2000) to the searching and self-critical commitment to pedagogical integrity (T. Groome, *Sharing Faith: The way of shared praxis*, San Francisco: Harper, 1991; J. Lee, ed., *Forging a Better RE in the Third Millennium*, Birmingham Ala.: RE Press, 2000). In whatever manifestation, confessional RE has a need to establish a pedagogical position of coherence and integrity, in which educational outcomes and intentions are clear, ethical and consistently pursued; this obligation applies as much to RE in confessional contexts as to community ones. The ways in which religious and belief communities can and must allow themselves to be transformed by educational processes are developed in Chapter 8.

37 Department for Education, *The Framework for the National Curriculum: A report by the expert panel for the national curriculum review*, London: DfE, 2011, pp. 42–3 and 60.

4 Phenomenology and anthropology: the advocacy of religion as an approach to RE

1 Ninian Smart, Foreword, in P. Connolly, ed., *Approaches to the Study of Religion*, London: Cassell, 1998, pp. xii–xiii.

2 So, for example, in J. Astley, L.J. Francis and M. Robbins, eds, *Peace of Violence: The ends of religion and education?* (Cardiff, University of Wales Press, 2007), the contributors are firmly wedded to Smart's approach to religion. When it is violent it is aberrant. As an example Jack Priestley states: 'Peace, I am suggesting is the agreed aim of all our religious quests' (p. 32) and that we need the courage to take on 'the distortions … that are being presented to the world as "real" religion, under the guise of which conflict and violence are breaking out all over the world' (p. 38.). This is an admirable aim but not in relation to the accurate representation of religion. It might also be argued that the failure of Western democracies to protect some of those states that are now experiencing violent fundamentalist religious reactions renders them somewhat culpable.

3 Ninian Smart, *The Science of Religion and the Sociology of Knowledge*, Princeton: Princeton University Press, 1973, p. 37.

4 Claude Lévi-Straus, *Tristes Tropiques* (trans. John and Doreen Weightman, 1974), London: Penguin, 1992 [1955], p. 386.

5 Lila Abu-Lughod, Do Muslim women really need saving? Anthropological reflections on cultural relativism and its others, *American Anthropologist*, 104 (3), September 2002, pp. 783–90, p. 785.

6 Hanna Papanek, Purdah in Pakistan: seclusion and modern occupations for women, in Hanna Papanek and Gail Minault, eds, *Separate Worlds*, Columbus, Mo.: South Asia Books, 1982, pp. 190–216.

7 Abu-Lughod, Do Muslim women really need saving?, p. 786.

8 This is not an epistemological question despite the fact it is often dressed up as such with recourse to the demands of scripture. Rather, we are talking here of different values paradigms, culturally contextualized and politically supported. The answer to the question is not to be found in any foundational authority but depends upon how we bring certain values constructions to the issue in question. To put it in another way, as addressed in Chapter 9, it is a pharmakonic matter. Whether women should be or not be veiled or covered is an undecidable based on the interpretation of the concept of modesty. When we disagree over this it is with a view as to what outcomes, in terms of rights, conventions and power relations will pertain as a result. To suggest that the status quo is to be affirmed by means of a favourable interpretation, 'mobile homes', is simply to ignore the wider issues that are brought into play when a particular society's values are considered in a larger

context. Educationally this sort of issue is also discussed in Chapter 9 in relation to the concept of *bricoleur*.

9 It should be pointed out that in the 2nd edition of her book on ethnographic fieldwork with Awlad 'Ali Bedouin families in the Western desert of Egypt (Lila Abu-Lughod, *Veiled Sentiments: Honour and poetry in a Bedouin society*, Berkeley, Calif.: University of California Press, 2000, p. xxi), she does discuss the issues that arise from ethnographic representation and the question of how these should be pursued but maintains, quite correctly, that without the representation itself these issues would be discussed in ignorance and through a distortive lens of reductive Western constructions; for example, in relation to the varied symbolisms of veiling within different Muslim influenced cultures and in relation to the concepts of modesty and honour.

10 Ruth Fremson, Allure must be covered: individuality peeks through, *New York Times*, 4 November 2001, p. 14.

11 Ibid.

12 Ibid.

13 Wilna A.J. Meier, *Tradition and Future of Islamic Education*, Munster: Waxman, 2006.

14 Saba Mahmood, *Politics of Piety: The Islamic revival and the feminist subject*, Princeton: Princeton University Press, 2005.

15 Ibid, p. 16.

16 Ibid, p. 17.

17 Ibid, p. 18.

18 Claude Lévi-Straus, *Tristes Tropiques*, p. 402.

19 Ibid, p. 403.

20 Ibid, p. 411.

21 Ibid, p. 149.

22 Philip Ball, who writes the *Guardian*'s critical scientist column, has put forward an interesting argument as to why religions need to be studied from a sociological point of view. He writes 'To decide to be uninterested in questions of how and why societies have religion, of why it has the many complexions that it does and how these compete, is a matter of personal taste. But to insist that these are pointless questions is to deny that this important aspect of human behaviour warrants scientific study. ... a single holy book can provide the basis for permissive enquiring and pro-scientific outlook or for apocalyptic, bigoted ignorance. ... Might we then, as good scientists, suspect that the real ills of religion originate not in the book itself, but elsewhere?' Philip Ball, Face to faith, *Guardian*, London and Manchester: Guardian Newspapers, 11 February 2012, p. 47. Ball is astute and sociological enquiry can be useful here but not in the sense that anthropological method has been exemplified above. The holy book can be interpreted in a number of ways to serve different ideological ends. In this sense it acts as a vehicle but it can also act as a source – this is also its value. Because of its 'holiness' it receives protective religious status. As a result different ideologies can be perpetrated through it with some impunity. The need to make value judgements upon the ideologies and their messages goes beyond the 'scientific' sociological remit and cannot ignore the role of religion as perpetrator any more than we can and have made judgements on other, secular, ideologies as they have manifested themselves, for example, in well known forms of communism and fascism.

23 One metaphor for recognizing the importance of socio-anthropological or ethnographic/ intercultural enquiry is provided by Eleanor Nesbitt, in saying that 'it provides a fine-grained, close up awareness' (Eleanor Nesbitt, *Intercultural Education: Ethnographic and religious approaches*, Brighton: Sussex Academic Press, 2004, p. 3). What I am also arguing for here is not just what we could describe as this closely but narrowly focused image with a long-range focal length lens to extract the detail, but also a wide-angle lens to capture the larger context. Nesbitt also, rightly, draws attention to the criticisms of Searle-Chatterjee, who states that 'we damage our understanding of society by defining and selecting out

'religion' and its assumed bearers' (Nesbitt, 2994, p. 8). However, the opposite could also be said to be true: that by not selecting out religion and identifying religions contextual socio-cultural influences we fail to recognize its ideological importance. To give a simple example, one 'assumed bearer' of authority, as Nesbitt describes them, might be a local priest/minister etc, another, in a larger global context, would be a revered pontiff or saint. We have to ask to what extent the messages of these authority figures influence the perceptions, values and practices of particular communities.

24 For a radically different assessment of Mother Teresa, for example, try Christopher Hitchens, *The Missionary Position: Mother Teresa in theory and practice*, London and New York: Verso, 1995.

25 See, for example, Karen Armstrong, *The Battle for God*, New York: Knopf, 2000, and *The Case for God: What religion really means*, London: Bodley Head, 2009.

26 Shlomo Sand, *The Invention of the Jewish People*, London: Verso, 2009, p. 14.

27 Ibid, p. 189.

28 Ibid.

29 See John Bowker, *Licensed Insanities: Religions and belief in God in the contemporary world*, London: Darton, Longman and Todd, 1987, pp. 9–24.

30 See for example, the delightful but disturbing personal account in Hugh Miles, *Playing Cards in Cairo: Mint tea, tarneeb and tales of the city*, London: Abacus, 2011.

31 Regis Debray, *God: An itinerary*, London and New York: Verso, 2004, p. 52.

5 Discourse and dissonance in contemporary paradigms of RE

1 Robert Jackson, *Rethinking Religious Education and Plurality: Issues in diversity and pedagogy*, London: RoutledgeFalmer, 2004, p. 165.

2 Ibid.

3 Ibid, p. 169.

4 Runnymede trust, *The Future of Multi-Ethnic Britain: The Parekh Report*, London: Profile Books, 2000, para 4.30, p. 53.

5 For example the 'radical postmodernist "personal narrative" approach' is ruled out by Jackson as not able to contribute to this dialogue because its 'anti-realist ideology suffuses its pedagogy, discriminating against children holding views of religious language, and depriving pupils of opportunities to scrutinize published resources introduced by the teacher', Jackson, *Rethinking Religious Education and Plurality*, p. 162.

6 Jackson, *Rethinking Religious Education and Plurality*, p. 166.

7 Ibid, pp. 121–2.

8 Ibid, Chapter 7, pp. 109–25.

9 Trevor Philips, 'Multiculturalism's legacy is "have a nice day" racism: the mere celebration of diversity does nothing to redress inequality', 2004, London and Manchester: *Guardian* Newspaper, 28 May. http://www.guardian.co.uk/society/2004/may/28/equality.raceintheuk (accessed 13 March 2011).

10 Nick Cohen, The secret scandal of Britain's caste system, *Observer* Newspaper, London and Manchester: Guardian Newspapers, 2011, p. 41. (26 June 2011).

11 Ibid.

12 Nick Cohen, *You Can't Read This Book: Censorship in an age of freedom*, London: Fourth Estate, 2012, p. 105.

13 Ibid.

14 Malise Ruthven, Divine revelation, *Guardian Review*, London and Manchester: Guardian Newspapers, 2011, p. 7 (02 July 2011).

15 James Barr, *Fundamentalism*, London: SCM Press, 1977. On pages 312 ff Barr refers to the fundamentalists' insistence that objectivity resides in scripture. This, of course, means that

any previous commentary on scripture can be superseded by being declared errant, it does not mean that the scripture itself is errant.

16 Ibid, p. 5.
17 Jonathan Romain, Face to faith, London and Manchester: *Guardian* Newspaper, 3 December 2011, p. 41.
18 Ibid.
19 Ibid.
20 See, for example Andrew Wright, The spiritual education project: cultivating spiritual and religious literacy through a critical pedagogy of religious education, in M. Grimmitt, ed, *Pedagogies of Religious Education*, Great Wakering: McCrimmons, 2000. Andrew Wright, *Critical Religious Education, Multiculturalism and the Pursuit of Truth*, Cardiff: University of Wales Press, 2007.
21. Andrew Wright, *Religion, Education and Postmodernity*, London and New York: Routledge Falmer, 2004, p. 231.
22. Andrew Wright, *Critical Religious Education, Multiculturalism and the Pursuit of Truth*, Cardiff: University of Wales Press, 2007.
23. Wright, Critical Religious Education, p. 1; Douglas Popora, *Landscapes of the Soul: The lack of moral meaning in American Life*, New York: Oxford University Press, 2001. p. 58.
24. Wright, *Critical Religious Education*; Popora, *Landscapes of the Soul*, pp. 57ff.
25. Wright, *Critical Religious Education*.
26. Wright, *Critical Religious Education*, p. 2.
27. It is worth noting that the last of these three reasons is the basis of the approach used by evangelists and salespeople alike: if you make it sound plausible as an overarching panacea for the inadequacy people experience in their lives then it's job done – whether the product is a (sub-prime?) bank loan or personal salvation.
28. Wight, *Religion, Education and Postmodernity*, p. 222.
29. Wright, *Religion, Education and Postmodernity*, p. 54.

6 The politics of English RE: a portrait of disfunctionality

1 Department for Education, Education Act, London: DfE, 1996, Section 390.
2 Department for Education, Education Act, London: DfE, 1996, Schedule 31 (7); Department for Children, Schools and Families (DCSF), *Religious Education in English Schools: Non-statutory guidance*, London: DCSF, 2010, pp. 10–11.
3 DCSF, *Religious Education in English Schools*, p. 12.
4 DCSF, *Religious Education in English Schools*, pp. 12–13.
5 DCSF, *Religious Education in English Schools*, pp. 10–13.
6 DCSF, *Religious Education in English Schools*, pp. 19–25.
7 DCSF, *Religious Education in English Schools*, p. 10, and Department for Education, *Education Act*, London: DfE, 1996, Schedule 31 (7).
8 Department for Education and Skills and Qualifications and Curriculum Authority, *Religious Education: The non-statutory national framework*, London: DfES and QCA, 2004, p. 12.
9 Ofsted, *Making Sense of Religion*, London: Ofsted, 2007, p. 34.
10 Ofsted, *Making Sense of Religion*, pp. 35 and 38–9; Ofsted, *Transforming RE*, London: Ofsted, 2010, pp. 4 and 7.
11 BBC and Culham College Institute, *Eggshells and Thunderbolts: RE and Christianity in the primary classroom*, Oxford: Culham College Institute, 1993, p. 10.
12 RSA, *Opening Minds*, London: RSA, 2010, http://www.rsaopeningminds.org.uk/about-rsa-openingminds/.

13　Department of Education, *Religious Education and Collective Worship*; Circular 1/94, 1994, p. 9; Department of Education, Education Act, London: DfE, 1993, Section 188 (6).

14　R. Alexander, ed., *Children, Their World, Their Education: Final report and recommendations of the Cambridge Primary Review*, London: Routledge, recommendation 50, pp. 494–5.

15　Department for Children, Schools and Families, *Religious Education in English Schools*, London: DCSF, 2010, pp. 14–16.

16　Department for Communities and Local Government, *Plain English Guide to the Localism Act*, London: DCLG, 2011, http://www.communities.gov.uk/publications/localgovern ment/localismplainenglishupdate.

17　J. Keast, *Religious Education in England: Still a critical time*, Self-published, 2011; M. Chater, *What's Worth Fighting for in RE?*, 2011, http://news.reonline.org.uk/re_news.php?355.

18　Ofsted, *Transforming RE*, London: Ofsted, 2010, p. 7; Ofsted, *Making Sense of Religion*, London: Ofsted, 2007, pp. 32–6.

19　National Association of Teachers of RE, Survey on EBac, www.natre.org.uk, 2011.

20　Department for Education, *The Framework for the National Curriculum: A report by the expert panel for the national curriculum review*, London: DfE, 2011, pp. 42–3.

21　Ibid, pp. 42 and 51.

22　Ibid, pp. 42–45 and 48.

7　The doors of pedagogical perception: pedagogy as existential stance

1　Jeffrey R. Di Leo and Walter R. Jacobs, eds, *If Classrooms Matter: Progressive visions of educational environments*, New York and London: Routledge, 2004.

2　Ibid, p. 2.

3　Ibid, p. 3.

4　Ibid.

5　Ibid, p. 1.

6　Henry A. Giroux, The Politics of Public Pedagogy, in Jeffrey R. Di Leo and Walter R. Jacobs, eds, *If Classrooms Matter: Progressive visions of educational environments*, New York and London: Routledge, 2004, p. 15.

7　Hampshire County Council, *Living Difference: Agreed syllabus for religious education*, Winchester: Hampshire County Council, Portsmouth City Council and Southampton City Council, 2004 and 2010 (revised).

8　C.Falk, sentencing learners to life: retrofitting the academy for the information age, theory, *Technology and Culture*, 22 (1–2), 1999, p. 7, http://www.ctheory.com/. See also, Erica L. McWilliam, Unlearning pedagogy, *Journal of Learning Design*, 1 (1), 2005, pp. 1–11, p. 4, http://eprints.qut.edu.au.

9　R. Alexander, *Introducing the Cambridge Primary Review: Children, their world, their education*, Cambridge: Esme Fairbairn Foundation, 2009, p. 19.

10　Hampshire County Council, *Living Difference*.

11　Ofsted, *Making Sense of Religion*, London: Ofsted, 2007, pp. 19–21; Ofsted, *Transforming Religious Education*, London: Ofsted, 2010, pp. 17–19.

12　Qualifications and Curriculum Authority, *Secondary Curriculum*, London: QCA, 2007, www.education.gov.uk/schools/teachingandlearning/curriculum/secondary.

13　J. Rose, *Independent Review of the Primary Curriculum: Final report*, London, DCSF, 2009, www.education.gov.uk/publications/eOrderingDownload/Primary_curriculum_Report.pdf.

14　J. Rose, *Independent Review of the Primary Curriculum*, pp. 54ff and 147ff.

15　R. Alexander, ed., *Children, Their World, Their Education: Final report and recommendations of the Cambridge primary review*, Abingdon: Routledge, 2010.

16　Jerome Bruner criticized some developmental theories – he did not have RE particularly in mind – as 'folk psychology' which is overly defining and prescriptive. He argued that developmental insights are needed 'to create in the young an appreciation of the fact that many worlds are possible, that meaning and reality are created not discovered.' (J. Bruner, *Actual Minds, Possible Worlds*, Boston, Mass.: Harvard University Press, 1986, p. 149.).

17 Hampshire County Council, *Living Difference*.

18 For further commentary on this see C. Erricker, *Religious Education: A conceptual and interdisciplinary approach for secondary level*, London and New York: Routledge/Fulton, 2010; C. Erricker, J. Lowndes, and E. Bellchambers, (2011) *Primary Religious Education – A New Approach: Conceptual enquiry in primary RE*, London and New York: Routledge/Fulton, 2011.

8 Towards an educational economy of religions

1 T. Cooling, Is God redundant in the classroom?, Inaugural Lecture at the National Institute for Christian Education Research, Christ Church Canterbury University, 2011.

2 K. Sporre and J. Mannberg, eds, *Values, Religions and Education in Changing Societies*, Dordrecht, London and New York: Springer, 2010.

3 R. Dearing, *The Way Ahead: Church of England schools in the new millennium*, London: Church House Publishing, 2001.

4 E. Humes, *Monkey Girl: Evolution, education, religion and the battle for America's soul*, San Francisco: Harper Collins Ebooks, 2007, p. 2.

5 J. Lawrence and R. Lee, *Inherit the Wind*, New York: Random House, 1951.

6 J. Orton and K. Weick, Loosely coupled systems: a reconceptualization, *Academy of Management Review*, 15 (2), pp. 203–23, http://www.jstor.org.pss/258154.

7 K. Weick, Educational organizations as loosely coupled systems, *Administrative Science Quarterly*, 21, 1976, pp. 1–19.

8 J. Moltmann, *The Trinity and the Kingdom*, London: SCM, 1981, p. 94.

9 K. Rahner, *The Trinity*, London: Burns and Oates, 1970, pp. 101ff.

10 It is clear that Augustine's educational thinking, as expressed in *De Doctrina Christiana*, was caught by an early form of this ambivalence (A. Augustine, *De Doctrina Christiana*, Oxford: Oxford University Press, 396, 1997, p. 117). In its mid-twentieth-century context, with Christian and modern Europe in crisis, the catechetical enterprise as interpreted by Jungman was employing essentially the same approach of wanting to use modern educational methods to imprint doctrine on children's minds (J. Jungmann, *Handing on the Faith: A manual of catechetics*, London: Burns and Oates, 1955.) Among contemporary church educators, there is a tentative, but wary recognition that catechesis needs forms of professionalism that the education system can provide (B. Roebben and M. Warren, eds, *Religious Education as Practical Theology: Essays in honour of Herman Lombaerts*, Leuven: Peeters, 2001) and an internal debate about how far, if at all, pedagogical perspectives should impact on Catholic truth (J. Conroy, ed. *Catholic Education: Inside out, outside in*, Dublin: Lindisfarne Books, 1999).

11 C. Brusselmans, *Toward Moral and Religious Maturity*, Morristown, N.J.: Silver Burdett.

12 J. Hull, *Studies in Religion and Education*, Lewes, Falmer Press, 1984; J. Astley, *The Philosophy of Christian Religious Education*, Birmingham, Al., Religious Education Press, 1994.

13 C. Richards, *Who Would a Teacher Be?* London: Darton, Longman and Todd, 1994.

14 J. Bruner, *Acts of Meaning: The Jerusalem–Harvard lectures*, Cambridge, Mass.: Harvard University Press, 1990, pp. 99–140.

15 Ibid, p. 5.

16 Ibid.

17 This authored self goes beyond the constructed religious self considered by Chris Hermans to be an outcome of good RE (C. Hermans, *Participatory Learning: Religious education in a*

globalizing society, Boston, Mass.: Brill, 2003, pp. 206ff). The self authored in our educational economy may or may not be religious, and may be either a teacher or a learner, or both.

18 P. Woods, Keys to the past and to the future, in D. Thomas, ed., *Teachers' Stories*, Buckingham: Open University Press, 1995, p. 189.

19 Department for Education and Skills, *Every Child Matters: Framework*, London: Stationery Office, 2003; Department of Children, Schools and families, *The Children's Plan: Building brighter futures*, London: DCSF, 2007. https://www.education.gov.uk/publications/standard/_arc_SOP/Page11/CM per cent207280.

20 M. Coles, *Every Muslim Child Matters*, Stoke on Trent: Trentham Books, 2008, pp. 131ff.

21 Ibid, p. 143.

22 R. Dearing, *The Way Ahead: Church of England schools in the new millennium*, London: Church House Publishing, 2001, pp. 11–12.

23 Ibid, pp. 11–12.

24 Ibid, p. 9.

25 P. Chadwick, *The Church School of the Future*, London: Archbishops' Council Education Division, 2012, pp. 36–8, recommendations 1 and 25.

26 M. Mayr, ed., *Does the Church Really Want Religious Education?* Birmingham, Al.: RE Press, 1988.

27 Ibid, p. 15.

28 Bishop John Pritchard is the Church of England Bishop of Oxford and Chair of the Church of England's Board of Education. His comments on children's voice and RE are in J. Pritchard, The greatest of these is ..., *Church Times*, 7768, London: Church of England, 3 February 2012, p. 23.

29 M. Gove, The *Today* Programme, BBC Radio 4, 20 January 2011.

30 Ibid.

31 The work of E.D. Hirsch in devising the US-based Core Knowledge curriculum includes a biblical literacy programme in which children should learn bible stories, in sequence, as part of their cultural literacy. E. Hirsch, *Core Knowledge*, www.coreknowledge.org 2012.

32 Pierre Bourdieu, Censorship and the Imposition of Form, in John B. Thompson, ed., *Language and Symbolic Power*, Cambridge, Mass.: Harvard Press, 1991:137.

33 See J. Derrida, *Of Grammatology*, Baltimore, Md.: John Hopkins University Press, 1974.

34 M. Gove, Ibid.

35 R. Alexander, ed., *Primary Children, Their World, Their Education: Final report and recommendations of the Cambridge Primary Review*, Abingdon: Routledge, 2010, p. 248.

36 Robert C. Post Censorship and Silencing, in Robert C. Prost, ed., *Censorship and Silencing: Practices of cultural regulation*, Los Angeles: The Getty Research Institute for the History of Art and the Humanities,1998: 6.

9 Between education and catastrophe: the futures of RE

1 See, for example, the way in which philosopher Alain de Botton exhorts atheists to use and adapt the resources of religious traditions rather than rejecting them outright: A. de Botton, *Religion for Atheists: A non-believer's guide to the uses of religion*, London: Hamish Hamilton, 2012.

2 K. Facer, *Education for Uncertain Futures*, London: RSA, 2011, www.thersa.org/events/video.

3 Jurgen Habermas, Philosopher as Stand-In and Interpreter, in J. Appleby, E. Covington, D. Hoyt, M. Latham and A. Sneider, eds, *Knowledge and Postmodernism in Historical Perspective*, London and New York: Routledge, 1996, pp. 514–15.

4 Jacques Derrida, Plato's Pharmacy, in *Dissemination*, London: Athlone Press, 1981.

5 Plato, *Phaedrus and the Seventh and Eighth Letters*, Harmondsworth: Penguin Books, 1973, pp. 274b–75b.
6 M. Taylor, *Twenty-first Century Enlightenment*, London: RSA, 2011, www.thersa.org/events/video.
7 Claude Lévi-Strauss, *The Savage Mind*, London: Weidenfeld and Nicolson, 1972, pp. 16–17.
8 Ibid.
9 Ibid. Derrida, in a critical appraisal, notes that Lévi-Strauss exempts engineers and scientists from his definition of *bricoleurs*. In other words they do not borrow from what is available to them but construct in origin their own discourse. In my view Derrida rightly states 'every finite discourse is bound by a certain *bricolage* and that the engineer and the scientist are also species of *bricoleurs*.' Jacques Derrida, Structure, Sign and Play in the Discourse of the Human Sciences, in Barry Stocker, ed., *Jacques Derrida: Basic Writings* London and New York: Routledge, 2007, p. 224. This would also agree with Kuhn's point on paradigms, above. One paradigm emerges out of the deficiencies of the previous one. It does not have its own origin ex-nihilo.
10 F. Inglis, *The Management of Ignorance: A political theory of the curriculum*, Oxford: Blackwell, 1985.
11 Ofsted, *Twenty Outstanding Primary Schools: Excelling against the odds*, London: Ofsted, 2009, p. 15.
12 M. Scott, *The Big Society Challenge*, Cardiff: Keystone Development Trust Publications, 2011, p. 202.
13 When we speak of truthfulness, we do not mean a commitment to the truth as formulated in any religion or philosophy. The imposition of 'the truth' in the form of pre-packaged, authoritative answers is a blight on RE. Truthfulness in the enquiry means a commitment to asking questions, and weighing up possible answers, with integrity, courage and reason. It says nothing at all about the destination of those enquiries.
14 T. Lickona, *Educating for Character: How our schools can teach respect and responsibility*, New York: Bantam Press, 1991.
15 See, for example, the emphasis on play in J. Kay, ed., *Good Practice in the Early Years* (London: Continuum, 2012), and the dimensions of successful learning specifically applied to early years and primary children, namely changing and learning, critical curiosity, meaning making and creativity, in the *Best Practice Network: Increasing learning power*, Bristol: Best Practice Network (2012, www.bestpracticenet.co.uk/content/increasing-learning-power).
16 Organization for Security and Cooperation in Europe, *Toledo Guiding Principles on Teaching about Religions and Beliefs in Public Schools*, Warsaw: OSCE Office for Democratic Institutions and Human Rights, 2007, www.osce.org/odihr/29154.

Index

capitalist 6, 13, 28, 40, 60, 113, 150

caste 67, 79–80, 86, 99, 130, 156

catechetical 125, 159

catechism 139

Catholic 86, 112, 125, 127, 159

chain of pedagogical development 108, 115, 118–20

chapels 132

children's rights 81

Christ 43, 45, 128

Christian 83, 92, 98, 100–1, 104, 123, 125, 144–8, 152, 159

Christian Aid 16

Christians 24, 80, 133

Church Dogmatics 23, 149

Church of England 17, 92–93, 127, 159–60

Church Times 149, 160

churches 16, 86, 132, 148

citizenship 1, 36, 51–2, 113, 116, 144, 149

City of London 15

city technology colleges 33

Cohen, Nick 79, 149, 156

Coles, Maurice Irfan 127, 160

collective worship 97–8, 158

Commentary on the Epistle to the Romans 23

Commission for Racial Equality 79

Communism 155

community cohesion i, 5, 21, 57–8, 76, 78, 97, 110, 141

confessional 7, 45, 48, 52, 55–7, 72, 83, 140, 152–4

confessionalism 153

confessionalists 56

confessionality 86

constructivist 120, 132, 141–2

contingency 110

Cooling, Trevor 78, 159

Copley, T. 153

Council of Europe 149

critical realism 84, 137

critical realist 56, 83

Culham College Institute 157

cultural relativism 61–2, 65, 154

curriculum i, 2, 5, 12, 17, 27, 30–1, 33–8, 46–8, 57, 75, 86, 94, 96, 102–3, 112, 118–20, 122, 133, 138, 141, 146, 150–2, 158, 160–1; agency 46, 99, 153; aims 30, 47, 94–5, 114, 116, 119;

authority i, 36, 151–4, 158; basic 51; breadth 115; constraint 77; content 37, 46–7; credentials 76, design 30, 36–8, 93, 96, 98, 102–3; documents 53, 102; hidden 150; idea 46, 133; issues 33; local 36, 151; managers 30; measures 32; models 47; national 27, 35, 30, 36, 53, 95, 98, 100–2, 118, 150–2, 154, 158; national definitions 116; obligations 100; panels 98; planning 38; policy 28, 118; politics 118–19; primary 30, 36, 118–19, 153, 158; progress 119; proposals 49; recognition 137; remit 46; representation of religion 23; RE 83, 142; review(s) 36, 38, 100, 154, 158; secondary 30, 36, 98, 118–19, 158; selection 47; school 30, 35, 39, 49, 144; structure 38, 119; subject(s) 3, 85, 96, 98; time 49; tools 95; whole 98, 120; wider 2, 98, 102–3, 116, 119; writers 37

Cush, Denise 78

Dearing Review 1993. 36

Dearing, R. Lord 22–4, 127, 159–60

Debray, Regis 71, 156

democracy/democracies 2, 6, 12, 14, 17–19, 21, 23, 60, 68, 72, 77, 134, 137, 146–7; capitalist 40; liberal 14, 66; parliamentary 52; spiritual 60; western 68–9, 154

democratic 23, 73, 77, 122, 131–2; anti 13, 17, 24, 32; citizens/ citizenship 112–13, 149; classroom 68; debate 111; dialogue 77; discourse 78; education 79, 114, 134; enquiry 17; environments 68; ethics 147; figures 72; goals 12; governance 23; government 147; ideal 21; institutions 161; integrity 103; Islam 66; laws 71; learning 114; narrative 13; order 13; participation 79; politics 33; principles 17–18, 21, 23; process 114; project 69; regulation 23, 71, 147; responsibilities 112; right(s) 13–14, 77–8; society(ies) 40, 69, 78–9, 111; spirit 66; state(s) 14, 17–18, 27, 31, 71; transparency 93; values 65, 72–3, 134; ways of life 87; West/ Western 12–13, 72; worldview 60

Derrida, Jacques 138, 139, 160–1